The **SAT** & PSAT Course Book

Math

SUMMIT
EDUCATIONAL
GROUP

Focusing on the Individual Student

The Eden Projects   Summit commits to planting a tree for every printed course book. Visit **edenprojects.org** to learn more.

Copyright Statement

The SAT & PSAT Course Book, along with all Summit Educational Group Course Materials, is protected by copyright. Under no circumstances may any Summit materials be reproduced, distributed, published, or licensed by any means.

Summit Educational Group reserves the right to refuse to sell materials to any individual, school, district, or organization that fails to comply with our copyright policies.

Third party materials used to supplement Summit Course Materials are subject to copyright protection vested in their respective publishers. These materials are likewise not reproducible under any circumstances.

Ownership of Trademarks

Summit Educational Group is the owner of the trademarks "Summit Educational Group" and the pictured Summit logo, as well as other marks that the Company may seek to use and protect from time to time in the ordinary course of business.

SAT is a trademark of the College Board.
PSAT is a trademark jointly owned by the College Board and the National Merit Scholarship.

All other trademarks referenced are the property of their respective owners.

CONTENTS

HEART OF ALGEBRA

PASSPORT TO ADVANCED MATH

ADDITIONAL TOPICS IN MATH

ANSWER KEY

Preface

Since 1988, when two Yale University graduates started Summit Educational Group, tens of thousands of students have benefited from Summit's innovative, comprehensive, and highly effective test preparation. You will, too.

Successful test-takers not only possess the necessary academic skills but also understand how to take the SAT. Through your SAT program, you'll learn both. You'll review and develop the academic skills you need, and you'll learn practical, powerful and up-to-date test-taking strategies.

The *Summit SAT & PSAT Course Book* provides the skills, strategies, and practice necessary for success on the SAT. The result of much research and revision, this book is the most effective, innovative, and comprehensive preparation tool available.

This book's first chapters – Test-Taking Fundamentals and Math Overview – give students a solid foundation of SAT information and general test-taking strategies. The following chapters cover the math content strands of the SAT – Problem Solving and Data Analysis, Heart of Algebra, Passport to Advanced Math, and Additional Topics in Math. Each chapter is divided into manageable topic modules. Modules consist of the skills, strategies, and common question types for particular topics, and *Put It Together* questions. At the end of each chapter, homework questions provide additional practice.

We are confident that you will not find a more complete or effective SAT program anywhere.

We value your feedback and are always striving to improve our materials. Please write to us with comments, questions, or suggestions for future editions at:

edits@mytutor.com

Your program will give you the skills, knowledge, and confidence you need to score your best.

Good luck, and have fun!

Chapter Summaries

We've reproduced the Chapter Summaries below to give you a preview of what you'll be covering. The Summaries are meant to serve as quick, condensed reference guides to the most important concepts. Obviously, you can't bring them into the test with you, but from now up until the night before the test, use them to preview and review the material covered in this book. Of course, Chapter Summaries also reside at the end of chapters.

General Test-Taking Summary

❑ Use the Two-Pass Approach.

❑ Focus on one question at a time.

❑ Write in your test booklet.

❑ Don't erase.

❑ Use process of elimination (POE).

❑ Check your work, quickly.

❑ Don't get tunnel vision. If you can't solve the problem in the forward direction, try to solve it in the reverse direction by plugging in the answer choices.

❑ Many SAT Math problems can be solved by choosing your own numbers for variables.

Problem Solving and Data Analysis Summary

❑ **Percent of a Number** – To find the percent of a number, convert the percent to a decimal and multiply.

❑ **Part/Whole** – To find what percent one number is of another, divide the part by the whole and then convert the resulting decimal to a percent. Remember the "is over of" rule.

❑ **Percent Increase/Decrease** – To find the percent increase or decrease from one number to another, divide the difference between the numbers by the original number, then convert the resulting decimal to a percent.

❑ **Multiple Percent Changes** – On percent questions that ask you to make two or more percent changes to a number, attack one change at a time. Don't just add or subtract the percents.

❑ **Rates as Ratios** – Ratios are a good way to express rates or some quantity "per" some other quantity. When comparing rates, reduce the fraction so you have 1 in the denominator.

❑ **Comparing Ratios** – To compare the ratios between multiple pairs of values, write the ratios as fractions and convert to common denominators.

❑ **Probability** – Probability of an event happening $= \dfrac{\text{\# of ways the event can happen}}{\text{\# of possible outcomes}}$

❑ **Proportions** – Solve proportions by cross-multiplying. If $\dfrac{a}{b} = \dfrac{c}{d}$, then $a \times d = b \times c$.

❑ **Rates** – Work completed $= \dfrac{\text{work rate}}{\text{time}}$

❑ **Dimensional Analysis** – Convert between units by multiplying by the units' conversion ratio. Set up the ratios so that your product is in the necessary unit and other units cancel. You may need to do multiple conversions to get the necessary unit.

❑ **Averages** – Average = $\dfrac{\text{sum of parts}}{\text{number of parts}}$

(average) × (number of parts) = sum of parts

❑ **Never Average Two Averages** – To find the average of two averages, you must first find the two subtotals, add them, and then divide by the combined number of parts.

❑ The **median** of a set of numbers is the middle number when the numbers are arranged in order. The **mode** of a set of numbers is the number that appears most frequently. The **range** of a set of numbers is the difference between the largest and smallest numbers. **Standard deviation** is a measure of how spread out the numbers are. The bigger the standard deviation, the more spread out the numbers are.

❑ When two variables have a **strong correlation**, their graph shows a clear trend. Variables with perfect correlation may appear as data points that lie precisely along a line. When two variables have a **weak correlation**, their graph shows a random cloud of points. When two variables have a **positive correlation**, one increases as the other increases. When two variables have a **negative correlation**, one increases as the other decreases.

❑ **Controlled Experiment** – A controlled experiment typically divides subjects into two groups – an experimental group and a control group. No treatment is given to the control group while the experimental group is changed according to some key variable. Otherwise, the two groups are kept under the same conditions.

❑ **Observational Study** – In an observational study, observations are conducted to monitor changes in variables. Investigators record data and analyze trends without giving any treatment to the variables.

❑ **Sample Survey** – In a survey, a sample from a larger population is selected and information from the sample is then generalized to the larger population. The key to the validity of any survey is randomness. Respondents to the survey must be chosen randomly. How well the sample represents the larger population is gauged by two important statistics: **margin of error** and **confidence level**.

Heart of Algebra Summary

❏ **Simplifying** – To simplify an algebraic expression, expand and combine like terms. To expand, you'll need to know the **Distributive Property** and the **FOIL** method.

❏ **Distributive Property** – When multiplying a single term by an expression inside parentheses, the single term must be multiplied by each term inside the parenthesis. When multiplying two binomials, each term must be multiplied by each term in the other binomial. Use the FOIL method: multiply the first terms, outside terms, inside terms, and last terms.

❏ **Factoring** – Factoring is expanding in reverse. In general, if you see something that can be factored, do it.

❏ **Equations** – Solve simple algebraic equations by manipulating the equation to isolate the variable.

❏ **Equations with Fractions** – If an equation contains fractions, clear them by multiplying both sides of the equation by a common denominator.

❏ **Solving for an Expression** – To solve for an expression, look for a quick way to manipulate the equation to generate the expression you're looking for.

❏ **Inequalities** – Inequalities can be solved like equations, with one important difference: if you multiply or divide both sides by a negative number, you must switch the direction of the inequality sign.

❏ **Absolute Value** – To solve an equation that has absolute value signs, remove the absolute value signs and set up 2 equations.

❏ **Systems of Linear Equations** – A system of linear equations, also called simultaneous equations, is a set of two or more equations working together. Simultaneous equations can be solved graphically and algebraically. A system of two linear equations can have no solution, 1 solution, or infinitely many solutions.

❏ **Elimination Method** – Add or subtract equations to cancel one of the variables and solve for the other. You may have to multiply an equation by some number to eliminate a variable before the equations are added or subtracted.

❏ **Substitution Method** – Solve one equation for one of the variables, and then substitute that value for that variables in the other equation.

❏ slope $= \dfrac{(y_2 - y_1)}{(x_2 - x_1)} = \dfrac{\text{rise}}{\text{run}}$

❏ **Parallel lines** have equal slopes. **Perpendicular lines** have slopes that are negative reciprocals of each other. **Vertical lines** have undefined slope. **Horizontal lines** have a slope of 0.

❏ The **slope-intercept form** of a linear equation is $y = mx + b$, where m is the slope of the line and b is the **y-intercept**. The y-intercept is where the line crosses the y-axis ($x = 0$ at the y-intercept).

❏ **Graphs of Systems of Equations** – When two lines intersect, the point of intersection represents the mutual solution of the lines. Algebraically, this is the graphical equivalent to solving a system of two linear equations.

❏ **Graphs of Inequalities** – To graph an inequality, change the inequality to an equation and graph the line. Then shade above or below the line depending on the direction of the inequality. For strict inequalities ($<$, $>$), use a dashed line; otherwise, use a solid line. The shaded region represents all solutions to the inequality.

❏ **Linear Models** – You can understand the meaning of variables by testing their effects. Also, it can be helpful to visualize a linear model as the graph of its line.

Passport to Advanced Math Summary

❑ **Equations with Fractions** – Fractions always make things more complicated. Look to clear fractions by using one of the following strategies:

1. Multiply the equation through by a common denominator – preferably the lowest common denominator.

2. If the equation is set up as a proportion, look to cross-multiply.

3. Simplify fractions with fractions in the denominator. Remember that dividing by a fraction is the same as multiplying by the reciprocal of the fraction.

❑ An expression is **undefined** when a denominator is equal to 0.

❑ **Solving for Variable in Exponent** – To solve an equation with a variable as an exponent, first make sure that each exponent has the same base. Then set the exponents equal to each other and solve.

❑ **Solving for a Variable Underneath a Radical Sign** – To solve an equation with a variable in a radical, isolate the variable and raise both sides of the equation to the appropriate exponent.

❑ **Evaluating Functions** – To evaluate a function, simply plug that value in everywhere you see an x.

❑ **Compound Functions** – A compound function is a combination of functions, usually written in a nested format like $f(g(x))$. This is described as "f of g of x." To evaluate a compound function, first evaluate the inner function and then plug that value into the outer function.

❑ Remember: y and $f(x)$ are the same. $f(x)$ is the y-coordinate of function f for a value x.

❑ **Factoring and Solving Quadratics** – Solve quadratic equations by following four simple steps.

1. Set the equation equal to 0.

2. Factor the equation.

3. Set each factor equal to 0.

4. Solve each of the resulting equations.

- ❑ **The Discriminant** – The discriminant is that part of the quadratic formula under the radical sign: $b^2 - 4ac$. You can use it to help you determine the types of solutions or roots the quadratic equation has.

- ❑ **Completing the Square** – If a quadratic equation is in standard form, you can convert it to vertex form by "completing the square."

  For an expression $x^2 + bx$, rewrite as $\left(x + \dfrac{b}{2}\right)^2$, then FOIL and rebalance the equation.

- ❑ **Polynomial Solutions** – A **solution** to a polynomial equation is also a **root** of the equation, a **zero** of the function, and an **x-intercept**. Any of these can be used to find a factor of the polynomial.
  Find the solutions of a polynomial by setting the polynomial equal to zero and factoring. Once in factored form, set each factor equal to zero to find the solutions. Consider group factoring if the usual factoring isn't working.

- ❑ **Dividing polynomials** – If a polynomial divides evenly into another polynomial, then both the divisor and the quotient are factors of the polynomial. If there is a remainder, then neither is a factor.

- ❑ **Exponential Relationship** – An exponential relationship is one in which the rate of change increases over time (exponential growth) or decreases over time (exponential decay). Algebraically, an exponential relationship is expressed as $y = ab^x$.

  In this form, for a typical SAT question, a is the initial value, b is the amount of change per unit of time, and x is the amount of time.

- ❑ **Quadratic Relationship** – A quadratic relationship first increases quickly, slows, and then decreases quickly, or vice versa. This is expressed algebraically as $y = ax^2 + bx + c$.

  In this form, for a typical SAT question, c is the initial value and x is the amount of time.

Additional Topics in Math Summary

- ☐ **Reference Information** – Do your best to memorize the formulas and rules given at the beginning of every SAT Math section.

- ☐ **Right angle** = 90°

- ☐ **Straight line angle** = 180°

- ☐ **Sum of interior angles of triangle** = 180°

- ☐ **Parallel Lines** – When a line crosses through parallel lines, it creates several sets of equal angles and supplementary angles.

- ☐ In an **isosceles** triangle, two sides are equal, and the two angles opposite those sides are equal.

- ☐ **Pythagorean Theorem**: $a^2 + b^2 = c^2$

- ☐ **Similar triangles** have corresponding angles that are equal and corresponding sides that are proportional. Similar triangles have the same shape but not necessarily the same size. Solve similar triangle questions by setting up a proportion of side lengths.

- ☐ **Area of Sector** = $\dfrac{x}{360}\left(\pi r^2\right)$

- ☐ **Length of Arc** = $\dfrac{x}{360}\left(2\pi r\right)$

- ☐ **Center-Radius Equation of a Circle**: $(x - h)^2 + (y - k)^2 = r^2$
  In this form, (h, k) is the center and r is the radius.

- ☐ **Completing the Square** – Not all circle equations are given in "center-radius" form. In those cases, you'll have to "Complete the Square" to get the equation into "center-radius" form.

- ❑ **SOH CAH TOA** is an acronym that represents the right triangle relationships for sine, cosine, and tangent.

  SOH: $\mathbf{S}\text{in}\,\theta = \dfrac{\text{length of }\mathbf{O}\text{pposite side}}{\text{length of }\mathbf{H}\text{ypotenuse}}$

  CAH: $\mathbf{C}\text{os}\,\theta = \dfrac{\text{length of }\mathbf{A}\text{djacent side}}{\text{length of }\mathbf{H}\text{ypotenuse}}$

  TOA: $\mathbf{T}\text{an}\,\theta = \dfrac{\text{length of }\mathbf{O}\text{pposite side}}{\text{length of }\mathbf{A}\text{djacent side}}$

- ❑ $\tan\theta = \dfrac{\sin\theta}{\cos\theta}$

- ❑ $\sin^2\theta + \cos^2\theta = 1$

- ❑ **Complementary angle identities:** $\cos A = \sin(90 - A)$ $\qquad\qquad$ $\sin A = \cos(90 - A)$

- ❑ **Degrees and Radians** – Angles can be measured in both degrees and radians. 180 degrees is equal to π radians.

  To convert from radians to degrees, multiply by $\dfrac{180}{\pi}$.

  To convert from degrees to radians multiply by $\dfrac{\pi}{180}$.

- ❑ When using your calculator, make sure it is in the right mode: degrees or radians. If you are working on a trigonometry question and your calculator shows an answer that doesn't seem to make sense, check whether you are in the right mode.

- ❑ **The Unit Circle** – You won't have to fully understand the unit circle, but you should know how to use the unit circle to find the sine and cosine of common angles.

- ❑ The square root of a negative number is called an **imaginary number**. Imaginary numbers are expressed using *i*, which is defined to be $\sqrt{-1}$. So, $i = \sqrt{-1}$.

- ❑ A **complex number** is any number that can be expressed in the form of $a + bi$, where *a* and *b* are real numbers. All real numbers and all imaginary numbers can be expressed as complex numbers.

Assessment and Objectives Worksheet

Complete this worksheet after the first session and refer back to it often. Amend it as necessary. It should act as a guide for how you and your tutor approach the program as a whole and how your sessions are structured.

The assessment will come from information that you and your parent(s) provide and from your initial diagnostic test. Keep in mind that you know yourself better than anyone else. Please be honest and open when answering the questions.

Student's Self-Assessment and Parent Assessment

- How do you feel about taking standardized tests? Consider your confidence and anxiety levels.

- Work through Table of Contents. Are there particular areas that stand out as areas for development?

- Other Concerns

Diagnostic Test Assessment

- Pacing

    - Did you run out of time on any or all sections? Did you feel rushed? Look for skipped questions or wrong answers toward the end of sections.

    - How will the concept of Setting Your Goal help you?

- Carelessness

    - Do you feel that carelessness is an issue? Look for wrong answers on easy questions.

    - Why do you think you make careless mistakes? Rushing? Not checking? Not reading the question carefully? Knowing "why" will allow you to attack the problem.

- Are certain areas for development evident from the diagnostic? Work through the questions you got wrong to further identify areas that might require attention.

Initial Score Goals

Note that score goals should be adjusted as necessary through the program.

Overall Goal: _____   Reading and Writing Goal: _____

Math Goal: _____   Essay Goal: _____

Program Objectives

Consider your assessment, and define your objectives. Make your objectives concrete and achievable.

Objective*	How to Achieve the Objective

*Sample Objectives

Objective	How to Achieve the Objective
Reduce carelessness by 75%.	Before starting to work on a question, repeat exactly what the question is asking.
Use Choosing Numbers and Plugging In fluently.	Tutor will point out all questions that are susceptible to these strategies. Note when a math question is susceptible to one or the other strategies.
Reduce test anxiety.	Build confidence and create a detailed testing plan. Start with easier questions to build confidence and slowly build toward more challenging questions. Take pride in successes and continue to reach for goals. Try to relax.
Improve calculator use.	Think about the question before jumping to the calculator. Have tutor hold on to calculator until it is needed.
Get excited about the test prep.	Stay positive. Know that score goals can be achieved. Learn tricks to beat the test. Make the test like a game. Focus on progress.

SUMMIT
EDUCATIONAL
GROUP

Test-Taking Fundamentals

- ❏ About the SAT

- ❏ Your SAT Program

- ❏ Your Commitment

- ❏ PSAT and SAT Test Structure

Introduction

Welcome! You are about to embark on a course that will empower you to reach your highest potential on the SAT.

About the SAT

What does the SAT measure? According to the College Board, it is a test of how well you've mastered important knowledge and skills in three key areas: reading, writing, and math. The College Board also says that an SAT score predicts how well you are likely to do in college and career. We feel that, to some extent, the SAT is a measure of how good you are at taking standardized tests. Either way, the SAT is an important element in the college admissions process.

Your SAT Program

Over the course of this program, you are going to learn to master the SAT by developing your test-taking abilities, working on fundamental SAT skills, and practicing with real SAT questions.

❑ Develop test-taking strategies.

Your instructor will emphasize both general test-taking strategies and problem-specific strategies. You will practice these techniques in session, during homework, and on practice tests. Our strategies make the SAT less intimidating and more like a challenging game.

❑ Build a strong foundation of skills.

You might need to review and practice skills in one or more topics that appear on the test. You might just be rusty, or the topic might be unfamiliar to you. Your diagnostic test, along with ongoing assessment, will uncover your areas for development. Over the course of your program, you and your tutor will work to strengthen these areas.

❑ Learn to recognize SAT question types.

While the SAT doesn't repeat exact questions from one test to another, it does repeat question types. After all, it's a standardized test. To help you become familiar with SAT question types and topics, you will work almost entirely with SAT-style questions. The ability to recognize question types allows you to be a proactive, rather than reactive, test-taker. You'll learn to see a question, recognize the topic and type, and immediately know what techniques and strategies to apply in order to solve it.

❑ Take practice tests under timed, real conditions.

Much like a scrimmage or a dress rehearsal, taking practice tests under realistic conditions removes the mystery of the test, helps reduce test anxiety, and increases your confidence. The experience of taking a practice test, combined with a thorough analysis and review of the test, forms the core of any successful test preparation program. We strongly recommend that you take 2 to 4 proctored practice tests during the course of your test prep program. Your tutor can help you schedule these.

❑ Review and rework the questions you get wrong, repeatedly.

This is the most powerful and simple tip for improving your SAT score. After a test is scored or a homework set is graded, it's natural to focus on the result and allow that score to dictate how you feel about yourself. Change this tendency, and instead view the test for what it is – feedback. What can I learn from this test? How can I use this test to improve? Dive into the test and focus on the questions you got wrong. For each question, note the question topic and type and work on the question until you can solve it. Don't just look at it and say, "Oh yeah, I know how to do that." <u>Write out the solution</u>. You'll learn it better.

But once is not enough! Review and rework these same questions <u>again and again</u> until you've mastered them. Make it part of every homework assignment. This process ensures that you're constantly reviewing and learning those topics and question types that are giving you trouble – a surefire path to a higher score.

Additionally, keep a notebook of techniques, rules, and formulas that are tripping you up. Review this list regularly.

Your Commitment

Your commitment to the program will determine how much you get out of it. Your instructor has made a commitment to your success on the SAT, and you need to make a commitment to helping yourself.

❑ Attend all sessions.

❑ Pay attention during sessions.

❑ Ask questions when you don't understand something.

❑ Complete all homework assignments.

❑ Take full-length, proctored practice tests.

SUMMIT
EDUCATIONAL
GROUP

PSAT and SAT Test Structure

The SAT is made up of four tests: Reading, Writing and Language, Math, and the Essay (which is optional). The Math Test is divided into two sections, one that allows a calculator and one that doesn't.

	PSAT	SAT
Format	4 Sections • 1 Reading • 1 Writing and Language • 2 Math 　- 1 No-Calculator Section 　- 1 Calculator Section	5 Sections (with essay) • 1 Reading • 1 Writing and Language • 2 Math 　- 1 No-Calculator Section 　- 1 Calculator Section • 1 Essay (optional)
Reading	60 minutes, 47 questions 5 passages Content: • Information and Ideas • Rhetoric • Synthesis	65 minutes, 52 questions 5 passages Content: • Information and Ideas • Rhetoric • Synthesis
Writing and Language	35 minutes, 44 questions 4 passages Content: • Expression of Ideas • Standard English Conventions	35 minutes, 44 questions 4 passages Content: • Expression of Ideas • Standard English Conventions
Math	70 minutes, 48 questions Content: • Problem Solving & Data Analysis • Heart of Algebra • Passport to Advanced Math • Additional Topics in Math	80 minutes, 58 questions Content: • Problem Solving & Data Analysis • Heart of Algebra • Passport to Advanced Math • Additional Topics in Math
Essay	No Essay	50 minutes, 1 prompt
Scoring	Evidence-Based Reading and Writing: 160-760 Math: 160-760	Evidence-Based Reading and Writing: 200-800 Math: 200-800 Essay: 6-24
Time	2 hours, 45 minutes	3 hours, 50 minutes (with essay)

SUMMIT
EDUCATIONAL
GROUP

Math Overview

- ❏ The SAT Math Test
- ❏ The PSAT Math Test
- ❏ Question Difficulty
- ❏ Scoring and Scaling
- ❏ Setting Your Goal
- ❏ The Instructions
- ❏ Working Through the Math Test
- ❏ Problem-Solving Tools
- ❏ Plugging In
- ❏ Choosing Numbers
- ❏ Using Your Calculator
- ❏ Grid-In Questions

The SAT Math Test

❑ There are 58 math questions that are split between a 25-minute no-calculator section and a 55-minute calculator section.

Format	58 questions
	Multiple-choice and grid-ins
	2 sections
	  - 1 with calculator NOT allowed (20 questions)
	  - 1 with calculator allowed (38 questions)

Content	Problem Solving and Data Analysis Heart of Algebra Passport to Advanced Math Additional Topics in Math
Scoring	Math score: 200-800

Time	80 minutes
	  - 25 minutes for no-calculator section
	  - 55 minutes for calculator section

❑ Each Math Test contains a specific number of questions in each of four content areas:

Content Area	Questions	Sample Topics
Problem Solving and Data Analysis	19	percents, proportions, statistics
Heart of Algebra	17	algebraic equations, systems of equations, graphs of linear equations, linear models
Passport to Advanced Math	16	functions, quadratic equations, polynomials
Additional Topics in Math	6	angles, triangles, circles, trigonometry, complex numbers

❑ Problem Solving and Data Analysis questions appear only in the 55-minute calculator-allowed section.

The PSAT Math Test

❏ There are 48 math questions that are split between a 25-minute no-calculator section and a 45-minute calculator section.

Format	48 questions Multiple-choice and Grid-ins 2 sections - 1 with calculator not allowed (17 questions) - 1 with calculator allowed (31 questions)
Content	Problem Solving and Data Analysis Heart of Algebra Passport to Advanced Math Additional Topics in Math
Scoring	Math score: 160-760
Time	70 minutes - 25 minutes for no-calculator section - 45 minutes for calculator section

❏ The PSAT and SAT are scored on vertically aligned scales. This means, for instance, that a student scoring 550 on the PSAT is demonstrating the same level of achievement as a student scoring 550 on the SAT. It does <u>not</u> mean that the same student is predicted to score a 550 on the SAT. The PSAT is reported on a slightly lower scale (160-760), reflecting the fact that the exams test the same body of skills, but at age-appropriate levels.

Question Difficulty

Problems progress in rough order of difficulty. You should always know whether you are working on an easy problem, a medium problem, or a difficult problem.

SAT Math Sections

25 Minutes – Calculator NOT Allowed

MULTIPLE-CHOICE														
1	2	3	4	5	6	7	8	9	10	11	12	13	14	15
EASY		→			MEDIUM			→			DIFFICULT			

GRID-INS				
16	17	18	19	20
E	→	M	→	D

> Note that the easy-to-difficult structure starts again with grid-ins. So, for instance, #16 will be much easier than #15. For some students, it is best to do the easier grid-ins <u>before</u> attempting the difficult multiple choice questions.

55 Minutes – Calculator Allowed

MULTIPLE-CHOICE																													
1	2	3	4	5	6	7	8	9	10	11	12	13	14	15	16	17	18	19	21	22	23	24	25	26	27	28	29	30
EASY					→						MEDIUM							→					DIFFICULT					

GRID-INS							
31	32	33	34	35	36	37	38
E		→		M		→	D

PSAT Math Sections

25 Minutes – Calculator NOT Allowed

MULTIPLE-CHOICE												
1	2	3	4	5	6	7	8	9	10	11	12	13
EASY		→		MEDIUM			→		DIFFICULT			

GRID-INS			
14	15	16	17
E	→	M	→ D

45 Minutes – Calculator Allowed

MULTIPLE-CHOICE																										
1	2	3	4	5	6	7	8	9	10	11	12	13	14	15	16	17	18	19	21	22	23	24	25	26	27
EASY			→					MEDIUM						→					DIFFICULT						

GRID-INS			
28	29	30	31
E	→	M	→ D

❑ **Use the structure of the test to your advantage**. Each question is worth 1 raw point. Regardless of its difficulty, every question counts the same. Would you rather earn $20 working for 1 hour or earn $20 working for 10 minutes? The answer is easy, right? Similarly, on the Math test, you should spend your time earning points as efficiently as you can.

Follow these tips:

- Put your time and energy into the questions within your capabilities, starting with the easiest and finishing with the hardest.

- Don't spend time on a hard question when there are easier questions still available. That's like passing on an opportunity to earn $20 in 10 minutes!

- When you're working on harder questions, make sure you check your answers! Suspect an answer that comes a little too easily.

- In each section, consider doing the first few grid-ins prior to doing the last few multiple-choice questions. But don't forget to go back to the multiple-choice questions you skipped!

❑ The questions in the calculator section are generally more complex than the questions in the no-calculator section. For some questions in the calculator section, your calculator can be a great help; however, some questions can be solved more quickly without a calculator.

Scoring and Scaling

You'll receive a Math section score from 200-800, a Math Test score from 10-40, and three subscores in Heart of Algebra, Problem Solving and Data Analysis, and Passport to Advanced Math. The subscores will be reported on a 1-15 scale. Some of the math questions will also count toward one of the two cross-test subscores called Analysis in Science and Analysis in History/Social Studies. College admissions offices will care most about the Math section score.

1 Total Score (400-1600 scale)	SAT			
2 Section Scores (200-800 scale)	Evidence-Based Reading & Writing		Math	
3 Test Scores (10-40 scale)	Reading	Writing & Language	Math	
2 Cross-Test Scores (10-40 scale)	Analysis in Science			
	Analysis in History / Social Studies			
7 Subscores (1-15 Scale)	Words in Context		Heart of Algebra	
	Command of Evidence		Passport to Advanced Mathematics	
		Expression of Ideas	Problem Solving & Data Analysis	
		Standard English Conventions		

- ❑ **How Your Score is Calculated** – You receive 1 raw point for a correct answer. You lose nothing for incorrect answers. Your **raw score** is calculated by adding up raw points. Your raw score is then converted to a scaled Math **test** score from 10-40 (8-38 for PSAT). This score is converted to a Math **section** score from 200-800 (160-760 for PSAT).

- ❑ **Never leave a question blank**. Since there is no penalty for wrong answers, you should answer every single question on the SAT.

Setting Your Goal

Set a goal. Envision where you want to be when you've finished your SAT preparation. Using your diagnostic results and previous test scores, work with your instructor to set a realistic score goal.

❑ Set your targets in the table below.

My Targets

My overall SAT Goal: _____

My Math Test Goal: _____

How many questions do I need to answer correctly (raw score)? _____

The Instructions

The instructions are the same on every SAT. Familiarize yourself with instructions before you take the test. At test time, you can skip the instructions and focus on the problems.

DIRECTIONS

For multiple-choice questions, solve each problem, choose the best answer from the choices provided, and fill in the corresponding circle on your answer sheet.

For grid-in questions, solve the problem and enter your answer in the grid on the answer sheet. Please refer to the directions on how to enter your answers in the grid.

NOTES

You may use any available space in your test booklet for scratch work.

1. The use of a calculator **is not permitted**. (a calculator is permitted on the 55-minute section)

2. All variables and expressions used represent real numbers unless otherwise indicated.

3. Figures provided in this test are drawn to scale unless otherwise indicated.

4. All figures lie in a plane unless otherwise indicated.

5. Unless otherwise indicated, the domain of a given function f is the set of all real numbers x for which $f(x)$ is a real number.

REFERENCE

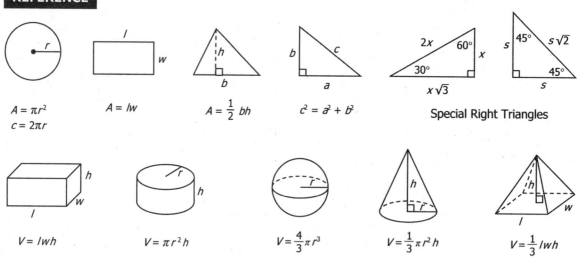

$A = \pi r^2$
$c = 2\pi r$

$A = lw$

$A = \frac{1}{2} bh$

$c^2 = a^2 + b^2$

Special Right Triangles

$V = lwh$

$V = \pi r^2 h$

$V = \frac{4}{3}\pi r^3$

$V = \frac{1}{3}\pi r^2 h$

$V = \frac{1}{3}lwh$

The number of degrees of arc in a circle is 360.
The number of radians of arc in a circle is 2π.
The sum of the measures in degrees of the angles of a triangle is 180.

Working Through the Math Test

❑ **Use the Two-Pass Approach.**

Step 1: On your first pass through a Math section, answer all of the questions you can, but don't get bogged down on an individual question. If you're stuck, mark it and move on. Remember: Each question is worth the same amount – 1 raw point.

On this first pass, remember that the first few grid-ins will be easier than the last few multiple-choice questions. If you get stuck on the harder multiple choice questions, move on to the easier grid-ins.

Step 2: Make a second pass through the test, starting from the first question you skipped and marked. Focus on the ones you think you have the best chance on. Use all of your math strategies.

Do as many of these as you can. For some, you will find the right answers. For the others, aggressively eliminate answer choices and make educated guesses.

Step 3: With 1 minute remaining, guess on all the remaining questions. Since there is no penalty for wrong answers, **do not leave any questions blank on your answer sheet**! You may temporarily leave questions blank while you're taking the test, but make sure every bubble is filled when time is called.

❑ **Focus on one question at a time**.

The SAT is timed, so it's normal to feel pressure to rush. Resist the temptation to think about the 10 questions ahead of you or the question you did a minute ago. Relax and focus on one question at a time. **Patience** on the SAT is what allows you to work more quickly and accurately.

Also, before you jump to the answers, reach for the calculator, or start scribbling things down, make sure you understand exactly what the question is asking.

Problem-Solving Tools

You need a set of several strategies for solving different types of SAT Math problems. Learn to adapt and try different strategies when you get stuck on a problem.

❏ **Write in your test booklet.**

You have space in the test booklet for a reason. Use it.

Be a proactive test-taker. Extract key pieces of information and write them down; write down the solution steps; draw a graph; make a table; label geometric figures; cross out incorrect answers. Practice this skill throughout your test preparation. You'll find yourself making fewer careless mistakes and clarifying solutions.

❏ **Don't erase.**

Don't waste time erasing calculations that you've mangled; just put a slash through them. It's faster.

❏ **Irrelevant information**

On rare occasions, an SAT math question will contain information that is not required to solve the question. If you've solved a question without using all of the information in the problem, it's very possible that you've done everything right.

❏ **Use process of elimination (POE).**

If you can't get to the right answer in a straightforward manner, look to eliminate answer choices. Consider the values and situation in the question, and eliminate answer choices that cannot logically work. The more answer choices you can eliminate, the greater advantage you have.

❑ **Check your work, quickly**.

Do a <u>quick</u> check after you do each question. Don't wait until the end of the section to check your work.

The test writers predict potential mistakes by students and include those mistakes as answer choices. These answer choices are considered "attractors" because they seem correct if you do not fully understand or fully solve the question.

Ask yourself:

- Did I find the number the question is asking for? Did you find x, but the question asks for $2x+4$? Did you find the radius, but the question asks for the diameter? Don't celebrate too soon!

- Can I quickly verify my answer? Can I use my calculator to verify? Can I plug in an answer choice to a given equation?

- Is my answer reasonable and logical given the context of the question?

For the following problem, determine how a student might arrive at each of the incorrect answer choices:

$$x - 2y = 2$$
$$2x + y = 9$$

For the system of equations shown above, what is the value of $x - y$?

A) −3
B) 1
C) 3
D) 4

How can you check your answer?

Why are 1 and 4 included as answer choices?

Why is −3 included as an answer choice?

Plugging In

As you progress through your preparation, you want to build your arsenal of SAT skills and strategies. Plugging In and Choosing Numbers are two of the most useful math strategies, providing you with a way to make abstract algebra questions more concrete and accessible, and allowing you to solve some very difficult questions.

❑ Don't get tunnel vision. If you can't solve the problem in the forward direction, try to solve it in the reverse direction by plugging in the answer choices.

> $y = -2x + 8$
> $3y = 5x + 13$
>
> Which ordered pair (x,y) satisfies the system of equations shown above?
>
> A) $(-1,10)$
> B) $(6,1)$
> C) $(1,6)$
> D) $(10,-1)$

❑ Plugging In can also be used on difficult word problems.

> Mrs. Stone brings some toys to her second-grade class. If each student takes 3 toys, there will be 10 toys left. If 4 students do not take a toy and the rest of the students take 4 toys each, there will be 1 toy left. How many toys did Mrs. Stone bring to the class?
>
> A) 40
> B) 74
> C) 85
> D) 91

Choosing Numbers

❑ Many SAT Math problems can be solved by choosing your own numbers for variables. We call this strategy Choosing Numbers. Learn to recognize questions that can be solved this way.

❑ Choosing Numbers is most effective on math problems whose answer choices contain variables, rather than constants. By Choosing Numbers, you'll be able to turn the algebraic expressions into hard numbers. Follow these steps:

1. Choose your own <u>easy</u> numbers to replace the variables. For problems that involve minutes or hours, for instance, you might try 60.

   For problems that involve percents you might try _____.

2. Solve the problem using your numbers.

3. Plug your numbers into **all** of the answer choices to see which answer choice(s) matches the solution you found in step 2.

4. If your numbers give you two or more correct answers, go back to step 1 and choose different numbers. You do not need to recalculate the choices you have already eliminated.

❑ Be careful to Choose Numbers that meet any restrictions in the question.

❑ Stay organized by writing down the numbers you choose and the answers you get.

The substance iodine-131 decays at a rate of 50% per 8 days. If a hospital stores 500 grams of iodine-131, which of the following represents the hospital's remaining stock after t days?

A) $0.5(500)^{\frac{t}{8}}$

B) $8(0.5)^{\frac{t}{500}}$

C) $500(8)^{\frac{t}{0.5}}$

D) $500(0.5)^{\frac{t}{8}}$

> When choosing numbers, use values that will work well with the situation in the question.
>
> Given a rate of 50% per 8 days, what numbers might you choose for t?

Choose a number for the number of days, t.

Given that number of days, how many times did the amount of iodine-131 decay by 50%?

Given that number of days, how many grams of iodine-131 would be remaining?

Substitute the number you chose for t into the answer choices. Which answer choice gives you the answer you arrived at in the previous question?

If a machine can fill s cartons in one 24-hour day, how many cartons can be filled in t hours?

A) $\dfrac{st}{24}$

B) $\dfrac{24s}{t}$

C) $\dfrac{t}{24s}$

D) $24st$

Using Your Calculator

You can use a calculator on only one of the two math sections, but even on that section fewer than half of the questions actually require a calculator.

Your calculator can help you compute more efficiently, handle fractions more easily, find points of intersection, and more.

A warning: **your calculator cannot solve problems for you; it is only a tool.** Your calculator is not always the right tool for the job. As you prepare for the SAT, learn to identify when the calculator is most useful and when it will just slow you down. Many questions in the calculator-allowed section do not require a calculator to solve.

❑ We recommend the TI-83 and TI-84 series of graphing calculators, which are widely used in American high schools. The following instructions are for those series of calculators. These calculators include functionality for fractions, trigonometric functions, and graphing. Although more advanced models exist, some of them are not permitted for use on the SAT.

Check the College Board website to see which calculator models are allowed for the test.

❑ Calculators follow strict order of operations. Use parentheses when entering a multi-step calculation, key numbers in carefully, and check the display after each entry.

Calculate each of the following, first without and then with a calculator.

> Use your calculator to solve:
>
> $-5^2 =$ _____ $(-5)^2 =$ _____ $\dfrac{-6 \times 20}{4 \times 5} =$ _____

❑ **Working with Fractions** – Use the ▶Frac function to convert decimals or complex fractions into simplified fractions. Press the MATH button; then choose ▶Frac by pressing either 1 or ENTER.

> Use your calculator to solve and put in simplest form:
>
> $\dfrac{2}{3} - \dfrac{1}{5} =$ _____ $\dfrac{52}{455} =$ _____

❑ **Graphing Functions** – Use your calculator's graphing function to find zeroes, intercepts, and points of intersection.

Graph the function $f(x) = x^2 - 4$.

Press the ⎡Y =⎤ button and enter your equation using the ⎡X,T,θ,n⎤ button for your independent variable.

Press ⎡GRAPH⎤ to see your function in the coordinate plane or ⎡2nd⎤ + ⎡GRAPH⎤ to see a table.

To change the x- and y-boundaries of the visible graph, press ⎡WINDOW⎤ and adjust accordingly.

Press ⎡TRACE⎤ and use the arrow keys to follow the coordinates on the line.

Press ⎡2nd⎤ and ⎡TRACE⎤ to bring up the CALC menu, and select the VALUE feature.

Enter any x-value to see its position and corresponding y-value.

What is the value of y when $x = 1.5$? _____

What are the coordinates of the function's x-intercepts? _____ _____

Find the intersections of $f(x) = x^2 - 4$ and $g(x) = x - 2$.

Enter both functions and graph them.

Press ⎡2nd⎤ and ⎡TRACE⎤ to bring up the CALC menu, and select the INTERSECT feature.

Use the up/down and ⎡ENTER⎤ keys to choose the two functions whose intercept(s) you wish to calculate, and use the left/right keys to select points near the intersection.

Press ⎡ENTER⎤ one more time to calculate the intersection.

How many times do $f(x)$ and $g(x)$ intersect? _____

What are the coordinates of the intersection(s)? _____

❑ While we can't list all the circumstances in which your calculator's advanced functions might be useful, it's worthwhile to explore its various menus and attempt to use your calculator in creative ways as you practice with SAT Math problems.

Grid-In Questions

13 of 58 math questions are grid-ins – 5 at the end of the no-calculator section and 8 at the end of the calculator section.

❑ Grid-in questions are just like the multiple-choice questions without the multiple choice answers.

❑ Grid-in questions progress from easy to difficult.

Remember that the easy-to-difficult structure starts again with grid-ins. The first grid-in question in a section will be much easier than the last multiple-choice question that comes before it. For some students, it is best to do the easier grid-ins before attempting the difficult multiple-choice questions.

❑ Although you should always write your answer in the boxes above the words, you receive credit only if the ovals are filled in correctly.

❑ Start gridding in the far left column to eliminate any indecision.

❑ Grid-in questions will not have negative numbers as answers.

❑ **Mixed numbers** must be gridded as improper fractions or decimals.

❑ **Decimals** must be gridded to the highest degree of accuracy possible.

In other words, an answer of 0.6666... should be gridded as .666 or .667 or 2/3. .66 or .67 will be marked wrong.

❑ Some grid-in questions may have more than one correct answer. You need to grid in only one of the correct answers.

❑ Check your work.

There are no answer choices to check your answers against, so make sure you check your work before you grid your answer.

Grid the following numbers.

0.7	$2\frac{2}{3}$ (grid as decimal)	$2\frac{2}{3}$ (grid as fraction)	π

SUMMIT
EDUCATIONAL
GROUP

Problem Solving and Data Analysis

- ❏ Percents

- ❏ Ratios

- ❏ Proportions

- ❏ Units and Conversion

- ❏ Statistics

- ❏ Data Relationships

- ❏ Data Collection and Conclusions

Percents – Part 1

❑ **Percent Conversions** – Percents, decimals, and fractions can all be used interchangeably. Almost always, you'll want to convert percentages to decimals so you can do the arithmetic. For instance, 22% of 110 should be written as 0.22 x 110.

Complete the table below.

Fraction			$\frac{1}{3}$	$\frac{1}{2}$		
Percent	10%				80%	
Decimal		0.20				1.2

❑ **Percent of a Number** – To find the percent of a number, convert the percent to a decimal and multiply.

> 22% of 110 is equal to _____

❑ **Part/Whole** – To find what percent one number is of another, divide the part by the whole and then convert the resulting decimal to a percent.

Remember the "is over of" rule. The number next to the "is" should go in the numerator (the part). The number next to the "of" should go in the denominator (the whole).

> 12 is what percent of 15? _____

❑ **Choose Numbers** – Some percent questions can be solved by Choosing Numbers. Try 100.

> SnacKrunch Chips sells "Reduced Sodium" potato chips with 20% less sodium than their regular chips. The company also sells "Salt & Vinegar" chips with 20% more sodium than their regular chips. The sodium content of the "Salt & Vinegar" chips is what percent of the sodium content of the "Reduced Sodium" chips?
>
> Choose a value for the sodium content of regular chips: _____
>
> What is the sodium content of "Reduced Sodium" chips? _____
>
> What is the sodium content of "Salt & Vinegar" chips? _____
>
> Use "Is Over Of" to compare the values.

PUT IT TOGETHER

Questions 1-2 refer to the following information.

The table below shows the results of a college student survey. Students were asked to provide their gender and major.

	Psychology	Mathematics	Business	Total
Male	190	46	184	420
Female	122	53	203	378
Total	312	99	387	798

1

Which of the following groups represents approximately 23% of the total number of people who responded to the survey?

A) Males majoring in business
B) Males majoring in psychology
C) Females majoring in psychology
D) Females majoring in business

2

Which of the following is closest to the percent of females surveyed who are majoring in mathematics?

A) 54%
B) 46%
C) 14%
D) 7%

3

Frank raises cattle for livestock. Last year, he sold exactly 30% of his cattle to a local rancher. If Frank has not gained or lost any cattle since last year, which of the following could be the total number of cattle he currently owns?

A) 610
B) 520
C) 350
D) 300

Percents – Part 2

- **Percent Increase/Decrease** – To find the percent increase or decrease from one number to another, divide the difference between the numbers by the original number, then convert the resulting decimal to a percent.

  The price of a printer is marked down from $200 to $150. What is the percent markdown in price?

- **Increasing (or Decreasing) by a Percent** – To change a number by a percent, find the percent of the number and then add it to (or subtract it from) the original number. You can also multiply the original number by 100% plus or minus the percent change.

  In 1993, the population of Butterdale increased by 16%. If the population was 12,025 at the beginning of the year, what was the population by the end of the year?

- Many percent word problems on the SAT require you to set up algebraic expressions or equations as part or all of the solution.

  Joshua pays an 18% tip on his lunch bill. Write an algebraic expression that represents Joshua's total bill, including tip.

  Choose a variable for Joshua's lunch bill: _____

  In terms of the variable, what is Joshua's tip? _____

  In terms of the variable, what is Joshua's total bill? _____

  A car repair shop charges a 12% markup on all parts used. If a bill charges a total of $691.88 for parts, what was the cost of the parts before the markup?

- **Multiple Percent Changes** – On percent questions that ask you to make two or more percent changes to a number, attack one change at a time. Don't just add or subtract the percents.

  A potential car buyer makes an offer for a car that is 80% of the sticker price. The salesperson makes a counteroffer that is 10% higher than the buyer's initial offer. What percent of the sticker price is the salesperson's counteroffer?

PUT IT TOGETHER

1

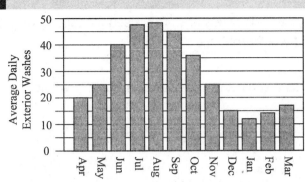

The chart above shows the average number of daily transactions at a car wash over the course of one year. Which of the following is closest to the percent increase in average daily exterior washes from May to June?

A) 15%

B) 37.5%

C) 60%

D) 62.5%

2

Students in a science class determine that a can of regular soda has an average of 5% more weight than a can of diet soda. Based on this information, if 24 cans of regular soda weigh 9576 grams, which of the following is the weight, to the nearest gram, of one can of diet soda?

A) 419 grams

B) 399 grams

C) 394 grams

D) 380 grams

> Use your calculator to work quickly and avoid careless mistakes on calculations involving large numbers.

3

A store increased the price of a computer by 10% and then discounted the computer by 30%. If the original price of the computer was p, and the price after the discount was c, what is the relationship between c and p?

A) $c = 0.2p$

B) $c = (1.1)(0.7)p$

C) $c = (0.1)(0.3)p$

D) $c = \dfrac{1.1p}{1.3p}$

> If you can't solve algebraically, try Choosing Numbers.

SUMMIT
EDUCATIONAL
GROUP

Ratios

A ratio compares one quantity to another. On the SAT, ratios are often used for rates (such as miles per hour or salary per year) in real-world word problems.

❑ **Ratio Basics** – A ratio can be thought of as a comparison between parts of a whole.

> A fruit basket contains 30 oranges and apples. The ratio of apples to oranges is 3 to 2.
>
> What is the ratio of oranges to apples? _____
>
> What fraction of the fruit in the basket is apples? _____
>
> How many apples are in the basket? _____
>
> If 5 pieces of fruit are randomly picked out of the basket, you would expect to get how many apples and how many oranges? _____

❑ **Rates as Ratios** – Ratios are a good way to express rates or some quantity "per" some other quantity. When comparing rates, reduce the fraction so you have 1 in the denominator.

> Which car goes faster? One that travels 150 miles in 5 hours or one that travels 120 miles in 3 hours?

❑ **Comparing Ratios** – To compare the ratios between multiple pairs of values, write the ratios as fractions and convert to common denominators.

> Thomas has a jar of 60 coins with 16 quarters. Sharon has a jar of 80 coins with 24 quarters. Who has the jar with the largest ratio of quarters to total coins?

❑ Probability of an event happening $= \dfrac{\text{\# of ways the event can happen}}{\text{\# of possible outcomes}}$

Probability questions typically involve data tables.

PUT IT TOGETHER

▼

Questions 1-2 refer to the following information.

A survey of 374 randomly selected people between age 18 and 41 years old gathered data on whether they have ever been married or not. The results are shown below.

	Have Married	Never Married	Total
18-23	36	84	120
24-29	54	36	90
30-35	79	27	106
36-41	51	7	58
Total	220	154	374

1

Based on the survey results, it is how many times as likely that someone aged 18-23 has married as it is that someone aged 24-29 has never married?

A) 4/3
B) 3/2
C) 1/1
D) 3/4

What is the probability that someone aged 18-23 has married?

What is the probability that someone aged 24-29 has never married?

Compare these two ratios.

2

Researchers acquired more survey responses. 9 more people aged 36-41 had been married, and a total of 4/5 of the people aged 36-41 had been married. Based on this information, how many of the additional respondents were aged 36-41 and had never married?

A) 5
B) 8
C) 12
D) 15

▲

3

Two competing stores offer different sale prices for the same snack item. ShopNow sells the snack in packs of 12 and has a sale offering 3 packs for $10. RitePrice sells the snack in packs of 6 and has a sale offering 4 packs for $7. Which store offers the lower sale price per snack item?

A) ShopNow has a lower sale price.
B) The sale prices are the same.
C) RitePrice has a lower sale price.
D) There is not enough information to determine the lower price.

Proportions

A proportion is a statement that two ratios are equivalent. $\dfrac{a}{b} = \dfrac{c}{d}$ is a proportion.

❑ When setting up a proportion, keep the same units in the numerators and the same units in the denominators.

$$\dfrac{60 \text{ miles}}{4 \text{ hours}} \text{ is equal to } \dfrac{15 \text{ miles}}{1 \text{ hour}}, \text{ NOT } \dfrac{15 \text{ hours}}{1 \text{ mile}}$$

❑ **Cross Multiplying** – Solve proportions by cross-multiplying. If $\dfrac{a}{b} = \dfrac{c}{d}$, then $a \times d = b \times c$.

> Solve for n:
>
> $\dfrac{3}{15} = \dfrac{n}{10}$ $\qquad\qquad$ $\dfrac{\$3.10}{1.2 \text{ min}} = \dfrac{\$n}{3.6 \text{ min}}$ $\qquad\qquad$ $\dfrac{n+3}{7} = \dfrac{n}{4}$

> In 2011, the average price to fill the 12-gallon fuel tank of a mid-size car was $42.24. At this price per gallon, what would be the cost of filling a large truck's 16-gallon tank?
>
> Set up the proportion: $\dfrac{42.24}{12} = \dfrac{x}{16}$
>
> Cross multiply and solve: ____ × ____ = ____ × ____

❑ **Rates** – Solve rate questions (also scale and recipe questions) by writing the rates as ratios and setting up proportions.

Work rate = $\dfrac{\text{work completed}}{\text{time}}$

> A geologist calculates that, due to tectonic forces, the North American continent moves 65 feet per 1000 years. At this rate, how long will it take for the continent to move 1000 feet?

PUT IT TOGETHER

A major snowstorm is expected to hit a ski resort at 2 PM. The storm is expected to last 8 hours with snow falling at a constant rate of 2.5 inches per hour. The resort currently has 48 inches of snow on the ground. How much total snow is the resort expected to have at 8 PM? (Assume any new snow will not compact any current snow.)

A) 48 inches
B) 50.5 inches
C) 63 inches
D) 68 inches

▼

Questions 2-3 refer to the following information.

Vitamin Content per 100 g	
B$_1$	0.24 mg
B$_2$	0.10 mg
B$_5$	11.44 mg
B$_6$	0.02 mg
E	9.09 mg

The data in the table above shows the average vitamin content per 100 grams of adult ostrich meat.

2

Of the following, which is closest to the expected amount of vitamin B$_1$ in 20 grams of adult ostrich meat?

A) 4.8 mg
B) 1.2 mg
C) 0.048 mg
D) 0.012 mg

3

The recommended daily intake of vitamin E for an adult male lion is 14.6 mg. Which of the following best approximates, to the nearest tenth of a gram, how much ostrich meat is needed to meet this amount of vitamin E?

A) 1606.2 g
B) 160.6 g
C) 1.6 g
D) 0.2 g

▲

Units and Conversion

Questions will often present data in one set of units (for example, km/hr) but ask for an answer in a different set of units (for example, km/min).

❏ **Metric System** – Know the following common metric conversion factors.

Metric Distance

10 millimeters = 1 centimeter   10 centimeters = 1 decimeter
10 decimeters = 1 meter   1000 meters = 1 kilometer

Common Metric prefixes

"milli-" is 1/1000th   "deci-" is 1/10th
"centi-" is 1/100th   "kilo-" is 1000

Other conversion factors

12 inches = 1 foot   3 feet = 1 yard
365 days = 1 year

❏ **Dimensional Analysis** – Dimensional analysis is a method for converting between and among different units using conversion factors. Convert between units by multiplying by the units' conversion ratio. Set up the ratios so that your product is in the necessary unit and other units cancel. You may need to do multiple conversions to get the necessary unit.

How many seconds are in 1.5 days?

$$1.5 \text{ days} \times \frac{24 \text{ hours}}{1 \text{ day}} \times \frac{60 \text{ minutes}}{1 \text{ hour}} \times \frac{60 \text{ seconds}}{1 \text{ minute}} = 129,600 \text{ seconds}$$

If there are 8 ounces in 1 cup, 2 cups in 1 pint, 2 pints in 1 quart, and 4 quarts in 1 gallon, how many ounces are in 2 gallons?

How many square centimeters are in 0.76 square meters?

PUT IT TOGETHER

1

Apothecary Measures

20 grains = 1 scruple	3 scruples = 1 dram
8 drams = 1 ounce	12 ounces = 1 pound

An apothecary calculates dosages of medication. Based on the information shown above, if the apothecary advises to take 48 grains per day for 30 days, this will be how much total medication in pounds?

A) 691.2
B) 120.0
C) 4.0
D) 0.25

2

The planet Mars travels 1,429,000,000 km in its orbit around the Sun. If it takes 1.88 years for Mars to complete its orbit, which of the following is closest to the average speed of Mars, in kilometers per hour, in its orbit around the Sun?

A) 2,082,483
B) 306,680
C) 163,128
D) 86,770

> Use your calculator for problems involving large numbers.

3

The California Aqueduct uses a pumping plant that pumps water at a rate of 5.56×10^7 cubic feet of water per hour. Of the following, which is closest to the plant's water pumping rate measured in cubic inches per hour?

A) 1.15×10^{12} cubic inches per hour
B) 9.61×10^{10} cubic inches per hour
C) 8.00×10^9 cubic inches per hour
D) 6.67×10^8 cubic inches per hour

Checkpoint Review

▼

Questions 1-3 refer to the following information.

Product	Price	Amount
L-Ribose	$88	500 mg
L-Galactose	$430	500 mg
L-Gulose	$213	100 mg
L-Erythrose	$128	100 mg
D-Threose	$62	50 mg

A company produces chemicals to be used by pharmaceutical manufacturers. The table above shows the prices of amounts of rare sugars.

1

How much more will 250 mg of L-Erythrose cost than 250 mg of L-Galactose?

A) $85
B) $95
C) $105
D) $115

2

D-Threose is created with 95% purity. If $1860 of D-Threose is purchased, it will contain what amount of pure D-Threose?

A) 1500 mg
B) 1425 mg
C) 150 mg
D) 145 mg

3

A customer orders a total of 3 g of L-Ribose and L-Gulose. If the total price of the order is $1505, how much L-Ribose, in grams, did the customer order?

A) 5 g
B) 2.5 g
C) 0.5 g
D) 0.25 g

▲

Checkpoint Review

▼

Questions 4-6 refer to the following information.

A survey was conducted annually among randomly chosen U.S. families to determine the number of cars owned per household. The table below shows the survey results.

	0 cars	1 car	2 cars	3+ cars	Total
1960	57	150	53	5	265
1970	55	160	91	14	320
1990	48	152	182	96	478
2010	56	147	243	142	588
Total	216	609	569	257	1651

4

What percent of the households surveyed in 1960 had exactly 2 cars?

A) 5%
B) 15%
C) 20%
D) 25%

5

In 2010, the total number of U.S. households was 117,600,000. Using the survey results, which of the following is the best estimate of the total number of households that owned no cars in 2010?

A) 42,800,000
B) 11,200,000
C) 2,800,000
D) 42,800

6

Based on the data, how many times more likely was it for a household in 2010 to own exactly 1 car than it was for a household in 1970 to own exactly 1 car?

A) 8 times as likely
B) 4 times as likely
C) 2 times as likely
D) 0.5 times as likely

▲

Statistics – Average (Mean)

The SAT requires you to know certain statistical terms like mean, median, mode, range, and standard deviation. Each of these values describes a set of numbers in a particular way. Mean, median, and mode are measures of the "central tendency" of a data set. Range and standard deviation, on the other hand, describe how spread out the numbers are. Questions involving these values often include charts and tables.

❑ Average = $\dfrac{\text{sum of parts}}{\text{number of parts}}$

> Over 5 days, the daily high temperatures in Cincinnati, Ohio, were 67°, 73°, 54°, 58°, and 63° Fahrenheit. What is the average high temperature for the five days?

❑ **ANT** – **A**verage x **N**umber = **T**otal – Occasionally, you'll be asked to calculate an average directly, but solutions to most average questions will require you to calculate the sum or total from a given average.

(average) × (number of parts) = sum of parts

> If the average of six numbers is 12, what is the sum of the six numbers? _____

❑ **Never Average Two Averages** – To find the average of two averages, you must first find the two subtotals, add them, and then divide by the combined number of parts.

> Three Gala apples have an average sugar content of 16 grams. Four Honeycrisp apples have an average sugar content of 23 grams. What is the average sugar content of all seven apples?
>
> What is the total sugar content for the Gala apples? _____ × _____ = _____
>
> What is the total sugar content for the Honeycrisp apples? _____ × _____ = _____
>
> What is the total sugar content for all the apples? _____
>
> What is the average sugar content for all the apples? _____

PUT IT TOGETHER

1

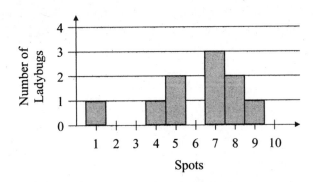

The histogram above shows the distribution of the numbers of spots on the shells of 10 ladybugs. Which of the following is the closest to the average (arithmetic mean) number of spots for the 10 ladybugs represented?

A) 5
B) 6
C) 7
D) 8

2

While out for a run, two joggers with an average age of 55 are joined by a group of three more joggers with an average age of m. If the average age of the group of five joggers is 43, which of the following must be true about the average age of the group of 3 joggers?

A) $m = 31$
B) $m > 43$
C) $m < 31$
D) $31 < m < 43$

3

During his history class, Mr. Johnson administers 5 tests. Each student receives a score between 0 and 100, inclusive. If a student in Mr. Johnson's class has an average score of 82 on the first 4 tests, what is the lowest score the student can score on the fifth test and still be able to have an average score of at least 80 for all 5 tests?

A) 12
B) 14
C) 72
D) 78

Statistics – Median, Mode, and Range

❑ The **median** of a set of numbers is the middle number when the numbers are arranged in order. If there is an even number of terms in a set, the median is the mean of the two middle numbers.

> List A consists of the numbers 12, 20, 15, 17, and 19.
> List B consists of List A as well as the numbers 24, 25, and 27.
>
> What is the median of List A? _____
>
> What is the median of List B? _____

❑ The **mode** of a set of numbers is the number that appears most frequently. Note that it is possible to have more than one mode in a list of numbers.

> What is the mode of the set {2, 35, 23, 37, 18, 37, 49, 8, 60, 1, 38, 17, 38}? _____

❑ The **range** of a set of numbers is the difference between the largest and smallest numbers.

> What is the range of the set {2, 35, 23, 37, 18, 37, 49, 8, 60, 1, 38, 17, 38}? _____

❑ **Standard deviation** is a measure of how spread out the numbers are. The bigger the standard deviation, the more spread out the numbers are. You will not have to calculate the actual standard deviation, but you have to understand the term.

> Is the standard deviation of {89, 90, 92} greater than, less than, or equal to the
> Standard deviation of {80, 90, 100}?

PUT IT TOGETHER

1

At summer camp, the median age of the campers is 12. If there are 9 campers, which of the following must be true?

I.   At least one of the campers is 12.
II. If there is an 11-year-old camper, there is also a 13-year-old.
III. The mode of the campers' ages is 12.

A) I only
B) I and II only
C) II and III only
D) I, II, and III

2

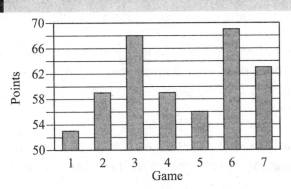

The Hilltop High School basketball team has played 7 games so far this season. The graph above shows the team's total points for each game. Based on this information, which of the following must be true?

I.   The mean is greater than the mode.
II. The median is greater than the mode.
III. The range is greater than the mean.

A) I only
B) II only
C) I and II only
D) I, II, and III

3

18.0	18.5	19.0	19.0	19.5	19.5
19.5	19.5	20.0	20.5	20.5	25.0

A random sample of 12 newborns had their height measured to the nearest half-inch, the results of which are shown above. However, the measurement of 25.0 inches is an error. Of the following, which will change the most when the 25.0-inch measurement is removed?

A) Mean
B) Median
C) Range
D) They will all change by the same amount.

Data Relationships

Graphs describe the relationship between two sets of data, such as weight versus height or distance versus time. Data relationship questions involve a variety of graphs, including scatter plots, line graphs, histograms, and bar graphs. Questions will ask you to make calculations, interpret trends, identify correlations, and make predictions.

❑ **Scatter Plot** – The scatter plot is the most commonly occurring graph on the SAT. A scatter plot gives you a graphical picture of corresponding data points.

When two variables have a **strong correlation**, their graph shows a clear trend. Variables with perfect correlation may appear as data points that lie precisely along a line. When two variables have a **weak correlation**, their graph shows a random cloud of points.

A **line of best fit** is a line that best represents the trend of data in a scatter plot. The line of best fit can be used to make predictions about points not on the graph. Algebraically, the line of best fit is expressed as $y = mx + b$, where m is the slope of the line and b is the y-intercept.

When two variables have a **positive correlation**, one increases as the other increases. When two variables have a **negative correlation**, one increases as the other decreases.

Distance (km)	Time (hrs)
7.1	1.2
4.5	7.0
6.8	4.3
7.6	0.9
3.3	8.8
5.0	5.5
6.2	3.6

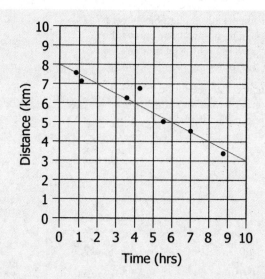

Does the data show a strong or weak correlation between distance and time?

Does the data show a positive or negative correlation between distance and time?

If time is equal to 12 hours, what is the likely value for distance?

❑ **Exponential Relationship** – The trend of scatter plot data is not always linear. An exponential relationship is one in which the rate of change increases over time (exponential growth) or decreases over time (exponential decay). Algebraically, an exponential relationship is expressed as $y = ab^x$.

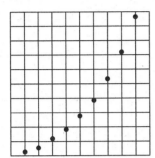

The graph shows the number of bacteria in a petri dish. The bacteria population grows by 30% every hour.

❑ **Line Graph** – Line graphs are like scatter plots in that they record individual data values as marks on the graph. The difference is that a line is created connecting each data point together. In this way, we can view more localized trends as well as the overall trend.

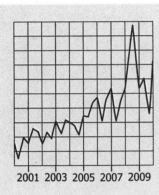

The graph shows the interest rates for a European nation from 2000 to 2010.

During which year did the interest rate show the largest increase?

Is the general trend increasing or decreasing?

PUT IT TOGETHER

Questions 1-2 refer to the following information.

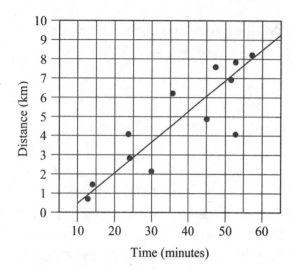

The scatterplot above shows a company's delivery times relative to the distance from the distribution center.

1

Based on the line of best fit to the data shown, which of the following values is closest to the average increase in time for an increase of 1 km delivery distance?

A) 25
B) 12.5
C) 6.25
D) 2.5

2

Based on the line of best fit, what is the predicted time for delivery to a home 5 km from the distribution center?

A) 35 minutes
B) 37 minutes
C) 40 minutes
D) 45 minutes

Questions 3-4 refer to the following information.

Document scan resolution determines image clarity and resulting file size. Scan resolutions (in dots per inch) and their resulting file sizes are shown in the graph below.

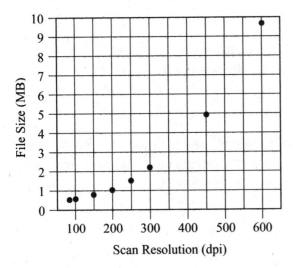

3

The trend established by this scatterplot closely resembles which type of function:

A) Linear
B) Logarithmic
C) Moving Average
D) Exponential

4

The best estimate for a file size based on a 400 dpi scan resolution would be:

A) 5.8 MB
B) 3.9 MB
C) 2.9 MB
D) 1.9 MB

5

Which of the following best describes an exponential relationship?

A) an athlete runs 10 miles every day
B) a savings account earns 2% interest annually
C) two business partners split profits in a ratio of 2:3
D) a student reads 1 more page a day than the previous day for 10 consecutive days

Data Collection and Conclusions

Data collection and conclusions questions ask you to consider how a study is conducted and what you can infer from the study's results. These questions deal with controlled experiments, observational studies, and sample surveys.

❑ **Controlled Experiment** – A controlled experiment typically divides subjects into two groups – an experimental group and a control group. No treatment is given to the control group while the experimental group is changed according to some key variable. Otherwise, the two groups are kept under the same conditions.

A control group is used to create a baseline to which experimental groups can be compared. If an experimental group shows results that a control group does not, it is likely that these results were caused by the variable that the experimenters manipulated.

❑ **Observational Study** – In an observational study, observations are conducted to monitor changes in variables. Investigators record data and analyze trends without giving any treatment to the variables.

Observational studies are used to determine the correlation between variables. Keep in mind that an association between two variables does not mean that changes in one variable cause changes in the other.

❑ **Sample Survey** – In a survey, a sample from a larger population is selected and information from the sample is then generalized to the larger population. The key to the validity of any survey is randomness. Respondents to the survey must be chosen randomly. How well the sample represents the larger population is gauged by two important statistics: **margin of error** and **confidence level**.

> Example: The Pew Research Center conducts a poll (survey) of 1000 voters, and 45% of the respondents say that they will vote for a Candidate Smith. The <u>confidence level</u> is given as 95% and the <u>margin of error</u> is given as 3%. This means that, if the poll were conducted 100 times, the percentage of voters who say that they will vote for Candidate Smith will range between 42% and 48% most (95 percent, actually) of the time.

Smaller sample sizes have larger margins of error. A sample size of 50, for instance, has a margin of error around 14%, while a sample size of 1000 has a margin of error around 3%. Similarly, the higher the desired confidence level, the larger the sample size needed.

PUT IT TOGETHER

1

A health official conducted a survey of the weights of random adult males in Oklahoma. A sample of 5,000 responses shows that the average weight was 176 pounds. The survey sample has a confidence level of 95% and a margin of error of 8 pounds. Which of the following is the most plausible value for the actual average weight of adult males in Oklahoma?

A) 165 pounds
B) 182 pounds
C) 186 pounds
D) 187 pounds

2

A scientist wants to study the effectiveness of an experimental medication for sinus congestion. The scientist records data on three groups of test subjects. The first group includes people who suffer from sinus congestion and are given the experimental medication. The second group includes people who suffer from sinus congestion and are not given the experimental medication. The third group includes people who do not suffer from sinus congestion and are given the experimental medication. Which of the following best describes the research design for this study?

A) Sample survey
B) Observational study
C) Controlled experiment
D) None of the above

3

A researcher conducting an observational study monitored the age, frequency of mating calls, and mass of male marsh frogs. The researcher observed that weight increased with age (approximately 1 gram per month) and calling rate differed among individual frogs but did not change with age. Based on this data, which conclusion regarding male marsh frogs is valid?

A) There is an association between age and calling rate.
B) There is no association between weight and calling rate.
C) An increase in weight causes a decrease in calling rate.
D) An increase in weight causes an increase in age.

Problem Solving and Data Analysis Summary

❑ **Percent of a Number** – To find the percent of a number, convert the percent to a decimal and multiply.

❑ **Part/Whole** – To find what percent one number is of another, divide the part by the whole and then convert the resulting decimal to a percent. Remember the "is over of" rule.

❑ **Percent Increase/Decrease** – To find the percent increase or decrease from one number to another, divide the difference between the numbers by the original number, then convert the resulting decimal to a percent.

❑ **Multiple Percent Changes** – On percent questions that ask you to make two or more percent changes to a number, attack one change at a time. Don't just add or subtract the percents.

❑ **Rates as Ratios** – Ratios are a good way to express rates or some quantity "per" some other quantity. When comparing rates, reduce the fraction so you have 1 in the denominator.

❑ **Comparing Ratios** – To compare the ratios between multiple pairs of values, write the ratios as fractions and convert to common denominators.

❑ **Probability** – Probability of an event happening $= \dfrac{\text{\# of ways the event can happen}}{\text{\# of possible outcomes}}$

❑ **Proportions** – Solve proportions by cross-multiplying. If $\dfrac{a}{b} = \dfrac{c}{d}$, then $a \times d = b \times c$.

❑ **Rates** – Work completed $= \dfrac{\text{work rate}}{\text{time}}$

❑ **Dimensional Analysis** – Convert between units by multiplying by the units' conversion ratio. Set up the ratios so that your product is in the necessary unit and other units cancel. You may need to do multiple conversions to get the necessary unit.

- **Averages** – Average $= \dfrac{\text{sum of parts}}{\text{number of parts}}$

  (average) $\times$ (number of parts) = sum of parts

- **Never Average Two Averages** – To find the average of two averages, you must first find the two subtotals, add them, and then divide by the combined number of parts.

- The **median** of a set of numbers is the middle number when the numbers are arranged in order. The **mode** of a set of numbers is the number that appears most frequently. The **range** of a set of numbers is the difference between the largest and smallest numbers. **Standard deviation** is a measure of how spread out the numbers are. The bigger the standard deviation, the more spread out the numbers are.

- When two variables have a **strong correlation**, their graph shows a clear trend. Variables with perfect correlation may appear as data points that lie precisely along a line. When two variables have a **weak correlation**, their graph shows a random cloud of points. When two variables have a **positive correlation**, one increases as the other increases. When two variables have a **negative correlation**, one increases as the other decreases.

- **Controlled Experiment** – A controlled experiment typically divides subjects into two groups – an experimental group and a control group. No treatment is given to the control group while the experimental group is changed according to some key variable. Otherwise, the two groups are kept under the same conditions.

- **Observational Study** – In an observational study, observations are conducted to monitor changes in variables. Investigators record data and analyze trends without giving any treatment to the variables.

- **Sample Survey** – In a survey, a sample from a larger population is selected and information from the sample is then generalized to the larger population. The key to the validity of any survey is randomness. Respondents to the survey must be chosen randomly. How well the sample represents the larger population is gauged by two important statistics: **margin of error** and **confidence level**.

Problem Solving and Data Analysis Practice

Percents

Questions 1-2:   E
Questions 3-4:   M

1

25% of 400 is equal to 20% of

A) 20
B) 80
C) 200
D) 500

2

	Red Marbles	Blue Marbles
Bag 1	2	3
Bag 2	3	7
Bag 3	4	8
Bag 4	5	12

In the bags above, Bags 1 through 4 contain only red and blue marbles. Which bag has the greatest percentage of red marbles?

A) Bag 1
B) Bag 2
C) Bag 3
D) Bag 4

3

Darya is an automobile engineer comparing a new type of brake pad, called Type N, to a more standard pad, known as Type S. On one type of road surface and at a certain driving speed, she finds that, on average, a typical driver's stopping distance is 10 percent greater when using Type N than when using Type S. If the average stopping distance with Type N is 176 feet, what is the average stopping distance in feet with Type S?

A) 155
B) 160
C) 166
D) 194

4

A computer hardware store has a stock of 70 desktop and 50 laptop computers. During a week, the store sells 20 percent of its desktop computers and 8 percent of its laptop computers. What percent of the total stock of computers was sold during this week?

A) 28%
B) 18%
C) 15%
D) 14%

Ratios

Question 5:   E
Question 6:   M
Question 7:   H

5

The effect of fish oil pills on intelligence was put to the test. Of 400 subjects, half were given fish oil pills and half were given a placebo (a pill with no active ingredients). After three months, the subjects were given intelligence and memory tests to see how many in each group improved.

	Showed Improvement	No Improvement	Total
Fish Oil	78	122	200
Placebo	64	136	200
Total	142	258	400

In the placebo group, what is the ratio of people who showed no improvement to those who showed improvement?

A) 8 to 17
B) 17 to 8
C) 8 to 25
D) 17 to 25

6

Two investors are to share profits of $14,000 in the ratio of 4:1. What is the amount of the smaller share?

A) $11,200
B) $5,600
C) $3,500
D) $2,800

7

A bag of 60 batteries in the ratio of 3 size D batteries to 7 size C batteries is combined with a bag having a ratio of 5 size D to 1 size C. If the two bags together now contain an equal number of size D and C batteries, how many batteries are in the second bag?

Proportions

Question 8:   E
Question 9:   M

8

Of every 300 chickens hatched at a farm, 120 will be kept as egg hens and 180 will be sold at market. At this rate, how many chickens will be sold if 750 chickens are hatched?

A) 300
B) 480
C) 450
D) 500

9

Machine A produces 150 widgets per hour. Machine B produces 200 widgets per hour. How many more minutes will it take Machine A than Machine B to produce 500 widgets?

A) 20
B) 25
C) 45
D) 50

Units and Conversion

Question 10:   E

10

| 1 kilometer = 1,000 meters |
| 100 centimeters = 1 meter |

Based on the equalities in the box above, how many centimeters are in 3 kilometers?

A) 0.003
B) 300
C) 30,000
D) 300,000

Statistics

Question 11:   E
Questions 12-14:   M
Question 15:   H

11

If the average of 8, 13, 21, and x is 15, what is the value of x?

A) 8
B) 12
C) 15
D) 18

12

Stuffed Animal	Price
Bear	$9.95
Elephant	$9.75
Monkey	$9.50
Rabbit	$8.25
Whale	$8.05

Cherie bought one of each of the five stuffed animals in the above list. What is the difference between the average (arithmetic mean) price per animal and the median price for the 5 stuffed animals?

A) $0.00
B) $0.10
C) $0.40
D) $9.10

13

Cathy	Ida	Kristy	Orrie	Stacy	Jasmine	Rosa
5' 9"	5' 6"	x	6' 0"	5' 6"	5' 11"	5' 5"

Based on the table above, if x is the median height for the team, which of the following could be Kristy's height?

A) 5' 5"
B) 5' 6"
C) 5' 9.5"
D) 5' 10"

14

In a set of nine different numbers, which of the following CANNOT affect the value of the median?

A) Increasing the smallest number only
B) Dividing each number by two
C) Decreasing each number by 20
D) Decreasing the smallest three numbers only

15

Over a period of 11 days, Seth counted a total of 143 customers in his father's diner. Throughout the 11-day period, exactly two more customers came in each day compared to the previous day. What was the difference between the average (arithmetic mean) number of customers per day and the median number of customers per day during the 11-day period?

Data Relationships

Questions 16-17:   E
Questions 18-19:   M

16

Which of the following graphs is the best example of a strong positive correlation between *h* and *w*?

A) *w*

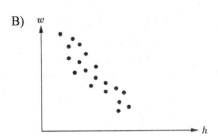

B) *w*

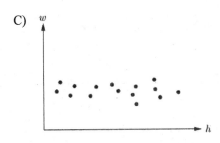

C) *w*

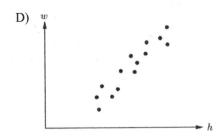

D) *w*

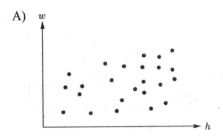

17

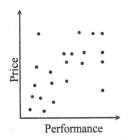

Which of the following is most likely the line of best fit for the scatterplot shown above?

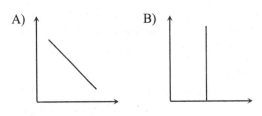

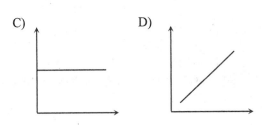

18

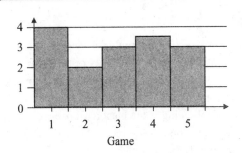

The chart above shows the number of fans in attendance for five college football games. If the total number of fans for all five games was 155,000, what is an appropriate label for the vertical axis?

A) Fans in attendance (in tens)
B) Fans in attendance (in hundreds)
C) Fans in attendance (in thousands)
D) Fans in attendance (in tens of thousands)

19

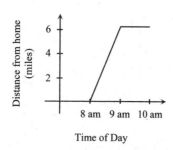

Time of Day

The graph above shows the distance of Ty's car from his home over a period of time on a particular day. Which of the situations below best fits the given information?

A) Ty drives from home to the dry cleaners and then returns home.

B) Ty is at the grocery store, takes the groceries home, and then drives back to the grocery store.

C) Ty leaves work, drives to a restaurant for lunch, and then drives back to work.

D) Ty leaves home, drives to work, and remains there.

Data Collection

Question 20:   E

20

A poll of 130 randomly selected editors found that 30% spent the majority of their career working from home. The results had a margin of error of 5% at a 90% confidence level. Which of the following is the most reasonable conclusion to draw about the percent of editors who work primarily from home?

A) Between 20% and 40% of editors work primarily from home.

B) Between 22% and 32% of editors work primarily from home.

C) Between 25% and 35% of editors work primarily from home.

D) Between 34% and 44% of editors work primarily from home.

Miscellaneous

Questions 21-22:   E
Questions 23-29:   M
Question 30:   H

21

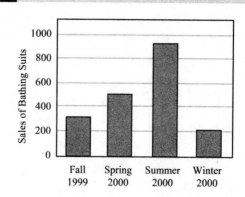

Consider the graph above based on the sales of bathing suits at Graham's Department Store. Based on the given data, what was the approximate percent increase from fall 1999 to summer 2000?

A) 100%

B) 200%

C) 300%

D) 400%

Category: _____

22

A gumball machine contains red, green, and white gumballs. If the machine is always stocked so there are twice as many red balls as green balls and twice as many green balls as white balls, what is the probability that a customer will get a red ball on a given purchase?

Category: _____

23

In 2001, snow accumulation in Canaan was 30% higher than it was in 2000. In 2002, snow accumulation for Canaan was 10% higher than it was in 2001. The snow accumulation in 2002 was what percent higher than it was in 2000?

A) 10%
B) 33%
C) 40%
D) 43%

Category: _____

24

The ratio of a to b to c to d to e is 1 to 2 to 3 to 4 to 5. If $c = 6000$, what is the value of e?

A) 1,000
B) 5,000
C) 10,000
D) 120,000

Category: _____

▼

Questions 25-26 refer to the following information.

The table below shows the results of a survey of a random sample of U.S. residents. They were asked if they used their cell phones primarily for sending or receiving text messages, making or receiving calls, or neither.

	Text	Call	Neither	Total
18-29	29,290	21,537	7,179	58,006
30-49	26,614	23,216	8,089	57,919
50-64	10,823	16,651	4,588	32,062
65+	4,383	9,862	3,702	17,947
Total	71,110	71,266	23,558	165,934

25

According to the survey results, for which age group did the greatest percentage of people report that they primarily used their cell phones to make or receive calls?

A) 18–29 year olds
B) 30–49 year olds
C) 50–64 year olds
D) 65+ year olds

Category: _____

26

A follow-up survey was conducted among 1,000 randomly chosen 30-49 year-olds who took the original survey and who reported they primarily used their cell phones for texting. They were asked if the people they texted most tended to be family members or not. Of these 1,000 people, 674 said that the people they text are mainly family members. Based on the original survey and this follow-up survey, which of the following is most likely to be an accurate statement about the survey population?

A) About 6,740 people 30 to 49 years old who primarily used their cell phones for texting texted mostly with family members.

B) About 18,000 people 30 to 49 years old who primarily used their cell phones for texting texted mostly with family members.

C) About 43,617 people 30 to 49 years old who primarily used their cell phones for texting texted mostly with family members.

D) About 48,000 people 30 to 49 years old who primarily used their cell phones for texting texted mostly with family members.

Category: _____

27

In 1998, there were approximately 69 million cell phone subscribers in the US. By 2005, that number had tripled. Assuming a constant rate of change, what is the best approximation for the number of cell phone subscribers in 2000 (in millions)?

A) 99
B) 109
C) 119
D) 129

Category: _____

Questions 28-29 refer to the following information.

An electrician is paid wages that are directly proportional to the number of lightbulbs he has screwed in. If he screws in 25 lightbulbs, he will make 175 dollars.

28

How many lightbulbs will the electrician have screwed in if he made 910 dollars?

A) 520
B) 260
C) 130
D) 65

Category: _____

29

The electrician must pay 26% of his wages as Union Dues, but the rest is his profit. What will be his profit if he screws in 65 lightbulbs?

A) 118.3 dollars
B) 336.7 dollars
C) 455 dollars
D) 1137.5 dollars

Category: _____

30

A city government representative wanted to research public opinion about building a new public library. The representative randomly selected 100 city employees for a survey. Of those surveyed, 84% supported the building of a new public library. Which of the following factors makes it least likely that the survey produced a reliable conclusion about the opinion of all people in the city?

A) The number of people who supported the building of a new public library
B) The pool from which the sample was selected
C) The population size
D) The sample size

Category: _____

SUMMIT
EDUCATIONAL
GROUP

- ❑ Algebraic Expressions

- ❑ Algebraic Equations & Inequalities

- ❑ Absolute Value

- ❑ Systems of Linear Equations

- ❑ Slope

- ❑ Graphs of Linear Equations

- ❑ Graphs of Linear Inequalities

- ❑ Creating Linear Models

- ❑ Interpreting Linear Models

Algebraic Expressions

Algebraic expression questions are relatively straightforward, typically requiring some degree of simplifying or factoring.

❑ An algebraic expression is an expression that includes one or more variables; it is not an equation. $-2(2x+3)$ is an algebraic expression.

❑ **Simplifying** – To simplify an algebraic expression, expand and combine like terms. To expand, you'll need to know the **Distributive Property** and the **FOIL** method.

> Simplify:
>
> $(k^2 - k + 4 + 2k - 3) - (k + 3k - 4) = $ _____

❑ **Distributive Property** – When multiplying a single term by an expression inside parentheses, the single term must be multiplied by each term inside the parentheses.

> $-3(2x^2 + x - 3) = $ _____

❑ **F.O.I.L.** – When multiplying two binomials, each term must be multiplied by each term in the other binomial. Use the FOIL method: multiply the first terms, outside terms, inside terms, and last terms.

> $(x - 1)(x + 5) = $ _____

❑ **Factoring** – Factoring is expanding in reverse. In general, if you see something that can be factored, do it.

> Factor:
>
> $(3x^4 - 12x^3 + 12x^2) = $ _____

Memorize the following quadratics.

$(a + b)^2 = \qquad (a + b)(a + b) = a^2 + ab + ba + b^2 \qquad = a^2 + 2ab + b^2$

$(a - b)^2 = \qquad (a - b)(a - b) = a^2 - ab - ba + (-b)^2 \qquad = a^2 - 2ab + b^2$

$(a + b)(a - b) = \qquad\qquad a^2 - ab + ba - b^2 \qquad\qquad = a^2 - b^2$

PUT IT TOGETHER

1

$$(-x^3y^2 - 4y^2 - 6x^2) - (-x^3y^2 + 4y^2 - 6x^2)$$

Which of the following expressions is equivalent to the expression shown above?

A) $-8y^2$

B) $8y^2$

C) $-2x^3y^2 - 12x^2$

D) $2x^3y^2 + 12x^2$

2

$$4x^4 - 16x^2y^2 + 16y^4$$

Which of the following expressions is equivalent to the expression shown above?

A) $\left(2x^2 - 4y^2\right)^2$

B) $\left(2x - 4y\right)^4$

C) $\left(x^2 - 2y^2\right)^2$

D) $\left(x^2 - 2y^2\right)^4$

3

$$-2(x + 5y)(3x - 3y)$$

Which of the following expressions is equivalent to the expression shown above?

A) $6\left(x^2 + 6xy - 5y^2\right)$

B) $6x\left(x^2 + 4xy - 5y^2\right)$

C) $6x(-x + y) - 30y(x - y)$

D) $6x(1 - y) + 30y(x - 1)$

Algebraic Equations & Inequalities

Simple equations and inequalities show up early in the test and don't require much more than basic manipulation.

❏ An equation is a statement that two expressions are equal. An equation must be kept balanced. If you do something to one side, you must do the same thing to the other side.

❏ Solve simple algebraic equations by manipulating the equation to isolate the variable.

> If $3x - 1 = 5$, what is the value of x?

❏ **Equations with Fractions** – If an equation contains fractions, clear them by multiplying both sides of the equation by a common denominator.

> If $\dfrac{3}{4}x + \dfrac{1}{2} = 5$, what is the value of x?

❏ **Solving for an Expression** – To solve for an expression, look for a quick way to manipulate the equation to generate the expression you're looking for.

> If $\dfrac{15 - a}{2} = 5$, what is the value of $15 - a$?

❏ If you're stuck, see if Plugging In can help.

❏ If you end up with an untrue statement after solving an equation, then the equation has no solution.

❑ An inequality is a statement that an expression is less than or greater than another expression.

❑ Inequalities can be solved like equations, with one important difference: if you multiply or divide both sides by a negative number, you must switch the direction of the inequality sign.

> Solve for x:
>
> $2 - 3x < 14$

❑ Some inequality problems can be solved by choosing numbers.

> Which of the following is the solution set for the inequality $2x - 1 > 5x + 8$?
>
> A) $x < -3$
> B) $x < -1$
> C) $x > 1$
> D) $x > 3$
>
> Does $x = 4$ satisfy the inequality? _____
>
> Does $x = -2$ satisfy the inequality? _____
>
> Does $x = -4$ satisfy the inequality? _____
>
> Which answer choice matches these results? _____

PUT IT TOGETHER

1

What is the value of h if $(h + 1) - (5h - 1) = 14$?

A) 3
B) 2
C) –2
D) –3

2

$$\frac{7(9+x)}{4} = \frac{(5+8x)+2}{6}$$

In the equation above, what is the value of x?

A) –35
B) –7
C) 7
D) 35

3

$$5p - 5 = 15 - 5p$$

Which of the following is the solution set to the equation shown above?

A) The equation has one solution, $p = -1$
B) The equation has one solution, $p = 2$
C) The equation has infinitely many solutions
D) The equation has no solutions

4

If $5 \leq 3 - 2h$, what is the greatest possible value of h?

A) 4
B) 2
C) 1
D) –1

5

$$5 + 3x < 3x - 2$$

Which of the following best describes the solutions to the inequality shown above?

A) $x > \dfrac{1}{3}$

B) $x < -\dfrac{1}{3}$

C) All real numbers

D) No solution

Absolute Value

❑ The absolute value of a number is the distance between the number and zero on the number line. It's probably easier, though, to think of absolute value as the "positive" value of the number.

> What does |2| equal? _____
>
> What does |−2| equal? _____
>
> If $x > 0$, then $|x| =$ _____
>
> If $x < 0$, then $|x| =$ _____

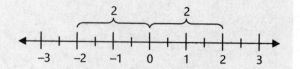

❑ Remember the positive and negative possibilities with absolute value.
For example, if $|x| = 2$, $x = 2$ or $x = -2$.

❑ To solve an equation that has absolute value signs, remove the absolute value signs and set up 2 equations.

> If $|x - 7| = 2$, what is the value of x?
>
> Positive possibility: _____
>
> Negative possibility: _____

❑ Most absolute value questions can be solved by Choosing Numbers or by Plugging In.

❑ If you like formulas, memorize the following to help you solve absolute value inequalities.

If $|algebraic\ expression| < a$, then $-a < algebraic\ expression < a$.

If $|algebraic\ expression| > a$, then $algebraic\ expression > a$ or $algebraic\ expression < -a$

> If $|x - 7| < 2$, what are the possible values of x? _____
>
> If $|x - 7| > 2$, what are the possible values of x? _____

PUT IT TOGETHER

1

$$1+|x+1|=0$$

What value of x satisfies the equation above?

A) -2
B) -1
C) 0
D) There is no such value of x.

2

On the number line, point Q has coordinate 2. Which of the following equations gives the coordinates of two different points on the number line that are both 5 units from point Q?

A) $|x-5|=2$

B) $|x+5|=2$

C) $|x-2|=5$

D) $|x+2|=5$

Systems of Linear Equations

Systems of linear equations appear frequently on the SAT. Most often, you are given a pair of equations and then asked to solve. Other times, the two equations are hidden in word problems, requiring you to set up the equations first and then solve. Systems of linear equations can be solved algebraically using the elimination method or substitution method. Some harder questions will present equations that have no solution or infinitely many solutions.

❑ A system of linear equations, also called simultaneous equations, is a set of two or more equations working together. Simultaneous equations can be solved graphically and algebraically. A system of two linear equations can have no solution, 1 solution, or infinitely many solutions.

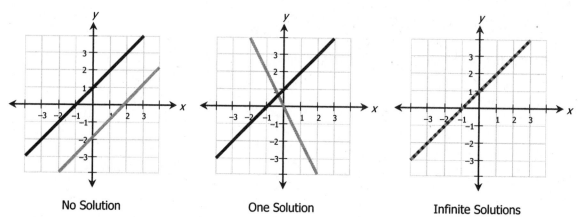

| No Solution | One Solution | Infinite Solutions |

❑ **No Solutions** – When lines are parallel, there is no common solution. What does this mean algebraically? If we consider the slope-intercept forms of the two lines ($y = mx + b$), it means that the slopes (m) are the same and the y-intercepts (b) are different.

❑ **Infinitely Many Solutions** – When lines overlap, there are infinitely many solutions. Algebraically, this means that the two lines have the same slopes (m) and the same y-intercepts (b).

> $2x + y = 5$
> $4x + 2y = 10$
>
> How many solutions does the pair of linear equations shown above have? _____
>
> How do you know?

❑ **Elimination Method** – Add or subtract equations to cancel one of the variables and solve for the other. You may have to multiply an equation by some number to eliminate a variable before the equations are added or subtracted.

> If $2x + y = 3$ and $-x - 3y = 6$, what is the value of y?
>
> Stack the equations: $2x + y = 3$
> $-x - 3y = 6$
>
> What do you need to multiply the bottom equation by to make the x disappear when you add the two equations? _____
>
> Rewrite the equations and add them. Solve for y.

❑ **Substitution Method** – Solve one equation for one of the variables, and then substitute that value for that variable in the other equation.

> If $2x + y = 3$ and $-x - 3y = 6$, what is the value of x?
>
> Solve the equation $2x + y = 3$ for y: _____
>
> Substitute that value for y in the other equation: $-x - 3(\underline{\hspace{2cm}}) = 6$
>
> Solve for x.

❑ **Simultaneous Equations in Word Problems** – Word problems that require you to define two variables are often simultaneous equation questions. Learn to recognize them and translate to set up the equations.

> A high school drama club is raising funds by selling t-shirts and sweaters. Club members sell t-shirts for $12 and sweaters for $25. If the club has sold a total of 16 items for $309, how many t-shirts have been sold?
>
> T = number of t-shirts sold
>
> S = _____
>
> Write an equation for the total number of items sold: T + S = 16
>
> Write an equation for the total revenue: _____
>
> Solve the simultaneous equations for T.

PUT IT TOGETHER

  1

$$2x + 2y = 2$$
$$x - y = 3$$

Consider the system of equations above. If (x, y) is the solution to the system, then what is the value of the product of x and y?

A) −12
B) −2
C) 1
D) 2

  2

$$\frac{1}{4}x + \frac{2}{3}y = 11$$

$$\frac{1}{2}x + \frac{1}{6}y = 8$$

Which ordered pair (x, y) satisfies the system of equations above?

A) (4,15)
B) (12,12)
C) (14,3)
D) (44,15)

> Solve both algebraically and by Plugging In answer choices.

3

The hardcover version of a book sells for $15 and the paperback sells for $11.50. If a store sells 70 copies of the book in one month and charges $917, how many hardcover versions were sold?

4

$$3x + ay = 80$$
$$x + by = 20$$

In the system of equations above, a and b are constants. If the system has no solutions, what is the value of $\dfrac{a}{b}$?

A) 12

B) 3

C) $\dfrac{4}{3}$

D) $\dfrac{1}{3}$

Checkpoint Review

1

If $\dfrac{x+2}{4} = h$ and $h = 4$, what is the value of x?

A) 0
B) 8
C) 14
D) 20

2

If $j \times k = 12$, what is the value of $3j \times 3k$?

A) 12
B) 36
C) 72
D) 108

3

If $4x + 3 = 27$, what is the value of $13x - 12$?

A) 77
B) 56
C) 45
D) 66

Checkpoint Review

4

$$2x + 3y = 7$$

$$\frac{1}{3}x + ay = 1$$

In the system of linear equations above, a is a constant. If the system has no solution, what is the value of a?

5

$$3m + 2n = 11$$
$$-6n - m = 7$$

What is the solution (m, n) to the system of equations above?

A) $(-2, 5)$
B) $(2, 5)$
C) $(3, 1)$
D) $(5, -2)$

Slope

❑ Slope is the amount a line moves vertically for every unit the line moves horizontally. Lines that slant up to the right have positive slope. Lines that slant down to the right have negative slope.

Algebraically, the slope of a line is given by:

$$\textbf{slope} = \frac{(y_2 - y_1)}{(x_2 - x_1)} = \frac{\textbf{rise}}{\textbf{run}}$$

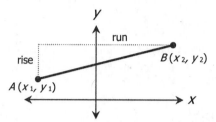

❑ **Parallel lines** have equal slopes.

❑ **Perpendicular lines** have slopes that are negative reciprocals of each other.

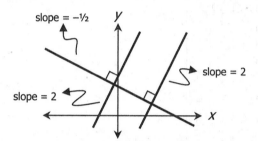

❑ **Vertical lines** have undefined slope.

❑ **Horizontal lines** have a slope of 0.

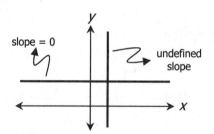

Find the slopes of the following:

$\overline{PR}$ _____

$\overline{QS}$ _____

Any line parallel to $\overline{PR}$ _____

Any line perpendicular to $\overline{PR}$ _____

Any line perpendicular to $\overline{QS}$ _____

PUT IT TOGETHER

1

A line in the *xy*-plane passes through the origin and has a slope of –0.5. Which of the following points lies on the line?

A) (–2,1)
B) (–2,–1)
C) (–1,–2)
D) (–1,2)

2

Two lines, *l* and *m*, are parallel in the *xy*-plane. Line *m* has an *x*-intercept of –4 and a *y*-intercept of 3. If line *l* has a *y*-intercept of –12, what is its *x*-intercept?

A) (0,9)
B) (9,0)
C) (0,16)
D) (16,0)

3

In the *xy*-plane, line *l* contains points in Quadrants III and IV, but not in Quadrants I or II. Based on this information, which of the following must be true about the slope of line *l*?

A) The slope is positive.
B) The slope is negative.
C) The slope is zero.
D) The slope is undefined.

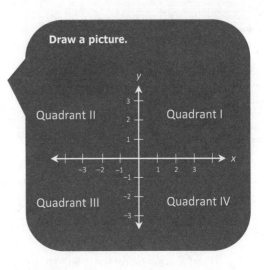

Draw a picture.

Graphs of Linear Equations

A line can be represented algebraically and graphically. The SAT requires that you understand the connection between the two.

❑ The standard form of a linear equation is **Ax + By = C**. A solution to the equation is a point (x, y) that satisfies the equation. Graphically, a solution is a point that lies on the line.

❑ The **slope-intercept form** of a linear equation is **y = mx + b**, where **m** is the slope of the line and **b** is the **y-intercept**. The y-intercept is where the line crosses the y-axis ($x = 0$ at the y-intercept).

❑ When you see a line in standard form, convert it to slope-intercept form.

> A line is given by the equation $6x - 2y = 7$.
>
> What form is the equation in? _____
>
> Write in slope-intercept form: _____
>
> What is the slope? _____
>
> What is the y-intercept? _____
>
> What is the x-intercept? _____
>
> Write an equation of a line that is parallel to the line: _____
>
> Write an equation of a line that is perpendicular to the line: _____

❑ To find the equation of a line when given two sets of points, first find the slope of the line. Next, write an equation $y = mx + b$ with the slope in place of m. Finally, plug in one of the points to the equation and solve for b.

> Find the equation for a line that passes through the points $(3, -1)$ and $(-5, 3)$.
>
> What is the slope? _____
>
> Write the equation in slope-intercept form: _____
>
> Plug in one of the points to solve for b.

❑ When two lines intersect, the point of intersection represents the mutual solution of the lines. Algebraically, this is the graphical equivalent to solving a system of two linear equations.

PUT IT TOGETHER

1

Which of the following graphs represents the equation
$3 + y = y + 2x - 1$?

A)

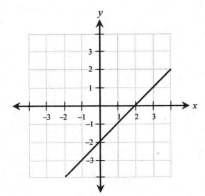

B)

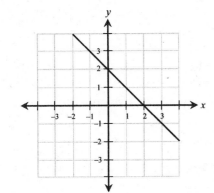

C)

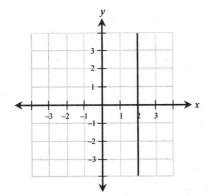

D)

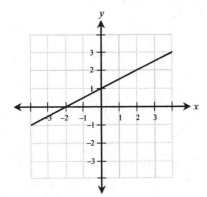

2

Which of the following best describes the graph of the equation $2x = \dfrac{1}{3}y - 1$ in the xy-plane?

Put in $y = mx + b$ form and sketch a graph of the equation.

A) The line has a positive slope and a negative y-intercept.
B) The line has a negative slope and a positive y-intercept.
C) The line has a positive y-intercept and a positive x-intercept.
D) The line has a positive y-intercept and a negative x-intercept.

 3

$$2x + y = -10$$
$$2y = x + 10$$

The equations shown above are graphed in the xy-plane. Which of the following must be true of the two equations?

A) The graphs of the two equations intersect at $(-10, 10)$.
B) The graphs of the two equations are the same line.
C) The graphs of the two equations are perpendicular lines.
D) The graphs of the two equations are parallel lines.

Questions 4-5 refer to the following information.

A hospital patient is receiving treatment for a low blood sugar level. The graph below shows the patient's blood sugar level S, in mg/dL, h hours after the treatment began.

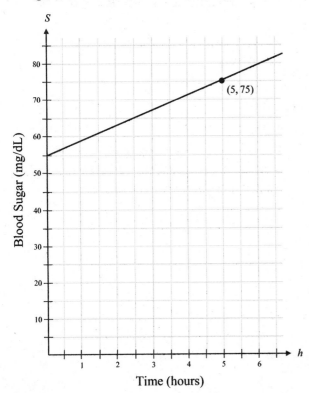

Time (hours)

4

Which of the following expresses the relationship between h and S?

A) $h = 4S$

B) $S = 6h$

C) $S = 4h + 55$

D) $S = \dfrac{1}{4}h + 55$

5

What does the S-intercept represent in the graph above?

A) The patient's blood sugar level at the start of treatment

B) The desired blood sugar level at the end of treatment

C) The total number of hours the treatment lasts

D) The increase in the patient's blood sugar level for each hour of treatment received

Graphs of Linear Inequalities

❑ To graph an inequality, change the inequality to an equation and graph the line. Then shade above or below the line depending on the direction of the inequality. For strict inequalities (<, >), use a dashed line; otherwise, use a solid line. The shaded region represents all solutions to the inequality.

Graph $y \leq 2x - 1$

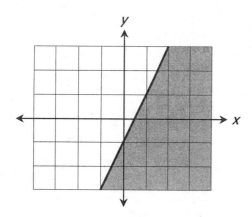

For the graph of this inequality, the line and the shaded region below the line make up all solutions.

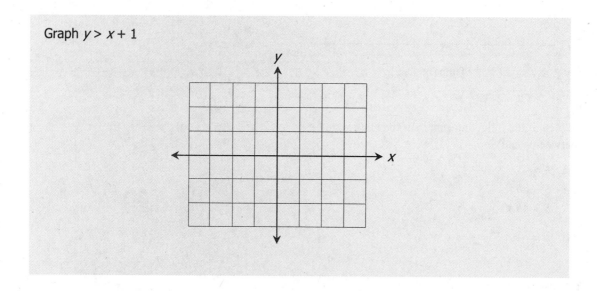

Graph $y > x + 1$

❑ You can solve some graphing inequalities problems by Plugging In or Choosing Numbers. Test values to see which coordinate points satisfy the inequality.

PUT IT TOGETHER

1

Which quadrant in the *xy*-plane contains no solution to the following system of inequalities?

$$y < \frac{1}{2}x + 1$$

$$y \le 3x - 2$$

A) Quadrant *I*
B) Quadrant *II*
C) Quadrant *III*
D) There are solutions in all four quadrants.

Creating Linear Models

One typical question type on the SAT is a word problem that describes a real world situation and then asks you to represent that situation algebraically with an expression, equation, or inequality (and sometimes a pair of equations or inequalities).

❏ Rewrite the definitions of the variables and identify the constants. Rewriting will help clarify the question.

> A cosmetics salesperson earns $10 per hour and a 22% commission for his sales. If a salesperson works for 7 hours and sells c dollars' worth of cosmetics, write an expression for the salesperson's earned income.
>
> How much did the salesperson earn without the commission? _____
>
> How many dollars' worth of cosmetics did the salesperson sell? _____
>
> How much did the salesperson earn from these sales? _____
>
> Write an expression for the salesperson's total earnings: _____

❏ Some linear model questions can be solved by Choosing Numbers.

> After summiting the top of a mountain that is 3000 feet in elevation, a hiker descends at a constant rate of 800 feet per hour. Which of the following best describes the hiker's elevation h hours after she begins her descent from the summit?
>
> What is the hiker's elevation before she begins her descent, when $h = 0$? _____
>
> What is the hiker's elevation after 2 hours, when $h = 2$? _____
>
> Which of the following answer choices matches this information?
>
> A) $f(h) = 800h - 3000$
>
> B) $f(h) = 2200h$
>
> C) $f(h) = 3000 - h$
>
> D) $f(h) = 3000 - 800h$

PUT IT TOGETHER

1

On a recent fishing trip, Art caught m fish each hour for 4 hours and Brian caught n fish each hour for 4 hours. Which of the following represents the total number of fish Art and Brian caught?

A) $4mn$
B) $4m + 4n$
C) $8mn$
D) $8m + 8n$

> Choose Numbers for m and n.

2

Lawrence is buying some new tools for his toolbox but only has $100 to spend. After buying three wrenches and two pliers, he still needs two screwdrivers. The wrenches cost $12 each and the pliers $14 each. If x represents the dollar amount he can spend on screwdrivers, which of the following inequalities could be used to determine possible values for x?

A) $(3)(12)+(2)(14)-x \leq 100$
B) $(3)(12)+(2)(14)-x \geq 100$
C) $(3)(12)+(2)(14)+x \leq 100$
D) $(3)(12)+(2)(14)+x \geq 100$

3

A doughnut shop has fixed daily costs of $750.00. Its variable costs come from doughnut ingredients, which average $0.23 per doughnut. If doughnuts are sold for $0.40 each, which of the following expressions could be used to predict the profit from producing d doughnuts in a single day?

A) $\$(0.40 - 0.23)d - \$750.00$
B) $\$750.00d + \$(0.40 - 0.23)$
C) $\$750.00 - \$(0.40 + 0.23)d$
D) $\$750.00 + \$(0.40 + 0.23)d$

Interpreting Linear Models

Linear model questions require that you understand clearly what slope and *y*-intercept mean in linear equations that represent real world situations.

- ❏ **Test Variables** – You can understand the meaning of variables by testing their effects.

    1. Choose Numbers for one variable and see how it affects other variables in the model.

    2. Using the definitions provided in the passage, determine what it means when a variable changes.

    3. Interpret the meaning of a constant by setting a variable to zero and isolating the constant.

    > The equation $d - 3 = 60h$ is used to express the distance d, in miles, of a train from a train station h hours after passing a rail switch.
    >
    > What does h represent? _____
    >
    > If h increases by 1, what happens to d? _____
    >
    > What does d represent? _____
    >
    > What does d equal when h equals 0? _____
    >
    > What does 3 represent? _____

❑ **Connect with Graph of Equation** – It can be helpful to visualize a linear model as the graph of its line.

1. If the given equation is not in slope-intercept form, rewrite it in the form of $y = mx + b$ so you can readily see what value is the slope and what value is the y-intercept. These are key numbers for understanding the model.

2. Rewrite the definitions of the variables.

3. Remember that the slope represents the amount the y, or dependent, variable changes per unit change in the x, or independent, variable. Typical x variables include units of time or money, like hours, years, or dollars.

4. Remember that the y-intercept represents the value of the y variable when the x variable is 0.

During a snowstorm, a meteorologist estimates the depth d, in inches, of snow on the ground in terms of the time t, in hours, from 1am to 6am, using the formula $d - 8 = 2t$. Based on the model, how many inches of snow are estimated to fall each hour?

Rewrite in $y = mx + b$ form: _____

What do the variables represent? $d =$ _____

$t =$ _____

Sketch a graph of the equation:

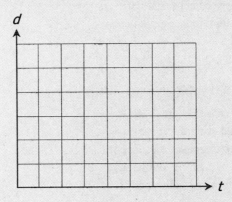

What number is the slope? _____

What does that number represent? _____

What number is the d-intercept? _____

What does that number represent? _____

PUT IT TOGETHER

1

Xin is a sculptor who brings her work to an art exhibit to sell. The number of sculptures that she has not yet sold can be estimated with the equation $S = 20 - 3h$, where S is the number of unsold sculptures and h is the number of hours since the exhibit opened. What is the meaning of the 20 in this equation?

A) Xin will sell all of her sculptures within twenty hours.
B) Xin arrives at the exhibition with twenty sculptures for sale.
C) Xin sells sculptures at a rate of twenty per hour.
D) Xin charges twenty dollars per sculpture.

2

Maria has planted a garden in her backyard. Her tomatoes are now ripe and she plans to pick them on a daily basis over the next week. The number of tomatoes left in the garden at the end of each day can be estimated with the equation $T = 98 - 14d$, where T is the number of tomatoes left and d is the number of days she has picked tomatoes. What is the meaning of the value 14 in this equation?

A) The number of tomatoes she plans to pick each day
B) The number of days she plans to pick tomatoes
C) The current number of tomatoes in her garden
D) The future number of tomatoes in her garden one week from now

3

The mean number of participants, y, in a city's adult baseball league can be estimated using the equation $y = 174.380 - 3.119x$, where x represents the number of years since 1990 and $x \leq 20$. Which of the following is the best interpretation of the number 3.119 in the context of this problem?

A) The estimated number of participants in 1990
B) The estimated yearly increase in the number of participants
C) The estimated number of participants in 2010
D) The estimated yearly decrease in the number of participants

4

$$0.1x + y = 12$$

The equation above models the gasoline consumption of a car with a gasoline capacity of 12 gallons over x miles, as well as showing how much gas that car will have left. What is the proper interpretation to the statement that (20, 10) is a solution to the equation?

A) That if you put 10 gallons of gasoline in the car, you can drive 20 miles.

B) That if you drive the car for 12 miles, 20 gallons of gasoline will have been used and 10 will be left over.

C) That the car always uses half of the gasoline that is has left in order to travel 20 miles.

D) That if you drive the car 20 miles, 10 gallons of gasoline will be left over.

Heart of Algebra Summary

- **Simplifying** – To simplify an algebraic expression, expand and combine like terms. To expand, you'll need to know the **Distributive Property** and the **FOIL** method.

- **Distributive Property** – When multiplying a single term by an expression inside parentheses, the single term must be multiplied by each term inside the parenthesis. When multiplying two binomials, each term must be multiplied by each term in the other binomial. Use the FOIL method: multiply the first terms, outside terms, inside terms, and last terms.

- **Factoring** – Factoring is expanding in reverse. In general, if you see something that can be factored, do it.

- **Equations** – Solve simple algebraic equations by manipulating the equation to isolate the variable.

- **Equations with Fractions** – If an equation contains fractions, clear them by multiplying both sides of the equation by a common denominator.

- **Solving for an Expression** – To solve for an expression, look for a quick way to manipulate the equation to generate the expression you're looking for.

- **Inequalities** – Inequalities can be solved like equations, with one important difference: if you multiply or divide both sides by a negative number, you must switch the direction of the inequality sign.

- **Absolute Value** – To solve an equation that has absolute value signs, remove the absolute value signs and set up 2 equations.

- **Systems of Linear Equations** – A system of linear equations, also called simultaneous equations, is a set of two or more equations working together. Simultaneous equations can be solved graphically and algebraically. A system of two linear equations can have no solution, 1 solution, or infinitely many solutions.

- **Elimination Method** – Add or subtract equations to cancel one of the variables and solve for the other. You may have to multiply an equation by some number to eliminate a variable before the equations are added or subtracted.

- **Substitution Method** – Solve one equation for one of the variables, and then substitute that value for that variable in the other equation.

- **Slope** $= \dfrac{(y_2 - y_1)}{(x_2 - x_1)} = \dfrac{\text{rise}}{\text{run}}$

- **Parallel lines** have equal slopes. **Perpendicular lines** have slopes that are negative reciprocals of each other. **Vertical lines** have undefined slope. **Horizontal lines** have a slope of 0.

- The **slope-intercept form** of a linear equation is $y = mx + b$, where m is the slope of the line and b is the **y-intercept**. The y-intercept is where the line crosses the y-axis ($x = 0$ at the y-intercept).

- **Graphs of Systems of Equations** – When two lines intersect, the point of intersection represents the mutual solution of the lines. Algebraically, this is the graphical equivalent to solving a system of two linear equations.

- **Graphs of Inequalities** – To graph an inequality, change the inequality to an equation and graph the line. Then shade above or below the line depending on the direction of the inequality. For strict inequalities ($<$, $>$), use a dashed line; otherwise, use a solid line. The shaded region represents all solutions to the inequality.

- **Linear Models** – You can understand the meaning of variables by testing their effects. Also, it can be helpful to visualize a linear model as the graph of its line.

SUMMIT
EDUCATIONAL
GROUP

Heart of Algebra Practice

Expressions

Questions 1-2:   E
Question 3:   M

1

Which of the following expressions is equal to $(6u^2v + 2v^2 - uv^2) - (3u^2v - uv^2 + 2v^2)$?

A) u^2v^2
B) $3u^2v + 4v^2 - 2uv^2$
C) $3u^2v$
D) $3u^2v + 4v^2$

2

$$(3k - 1)^2$$

Which of the following is equivalent to the expression shown above?

A) $9k^2 + 1$
B) $9k^2 - 6k + 1$
C) $9k^2 - 1$
D) $9k^2 - 6k - 1$

3

$$16x^4 + 16x^2y + 4y^2$$

Which of the following is equivalent to the expression above?

A) $\left(4x^2 + 2y\right)^2$

B) $\left(16x^2 + 8y\right)^2$

C) $\left(4x^2 + 2y\right)\left(4x^2 - 2y\right)$

D) $\left(x^4 + y\right)\left(4x - y\right)$

Equations and Inequalities

Questions 4-5:   E

4

If $3x + 7 \geq 20$, then which of the following must be true of the value of x?

A) $x < 0$
B) $x \neq 6$
C) $x \geq 5$
D) $x > 4$

5

If $3a + a = 12$, what is the value of $3a - a$?

Absolute Value

Question 6:   E

6

What value of n makes $|n - 2| + 4 = 0$?

A) -2
B) 2
C) 6
D) There is no such value of n.

Systems of Linear Equations

Questions 7-8:   E
Questions 9-10:   M

7

$$5x - 4y = -3$$
$$3y - 4x = 7$$

Identify the value of $x - y$.

A) $-\dfrac{2}{5}$

B) $\dfrac{3}{5}$

C) $\dfrac{5}{4}$

D) 4

8

At a certain department store, 3 skirts and 5 tops cost $90, while 3 skirts and 2 tops cost $63. Assuming all skirts are priced the same and all tops are priced the same, what is the cost of 1 top?

A) $4.50
B) $9.00
C) $15.00
D) $27.00

9

$$y \geq 2x + a$$
$$y < -2x + b$$

In the xy-plane, if $(1,0)$ is a solution to the system of inequalities shown above, where a and b are constants, which of the following must be true?

A) $a < b$
B) $b < a$
C) $a = -b$
D) $|a| < |b|$

10

$$r = 7.25 - 0.05x$$
$$b = 10.25 - 0.15x$$

The equations above represent the daily electricity usage of Rasheed and Beth during a 2-month period of last year, where r and b represent the daily usage in kWh (kilowatt hours) for Rasheed and Beth, respectively, and x is the number of days since October 1. How many kWh did each person use when their electricity usages were equal?

A) 0.55
B) 4.25
C) 5.50
D) 5.75

Slope

Questions 11-12:   E

11

In the xy-plane, what is the slope of the line that passes through points $(-1, 4)$ and $(3, -2)$?

A) $-\dfrac{3}{2}$

B) $-\dfrac{2}{3}$

C) $\dfrac{2}{3}$

D) $\dfrac{3}{2}$

12

If a line in the xy-plane passes through the point $(0, 1)$ and has slope $\dfrac{1}{2}$, which of the following points is also on the line?

A) $(0, 3)$
B) $(1, 2)$
C) $(1, 3)$
D) $(4, 3)$

Graphs of Linear Equations

Question 13:   M
Question 14:   H

13

The graph of a line in the xy-plane has slope -3 and y-intercept 3. The graph of a second line has slope 3 and y-intercept -9. At what point do the two lines intersect?

A) $(-3, -2)$
B) $(-3, 2)$
C) $(2, -3)$
D) $(2, 3)$

SUMMIT
EDUCATIONAL
GROUP

14

The graph of a line passes through the point $(1, 2)$ and has a slope of 5. Another line passes through the points $(5, 0)$ and $(-1, 2)$. The two lines intersect at point (p, q). What is the value of $\dfrac{p}{q}$?

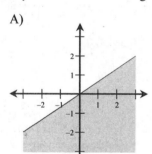

Graphs of Inequalities

Question 15:   M

15

Which of the following best represents the graph of $y \le ax + b$ for some negative a and negative b?

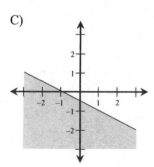

A)

B)

C)

D)

Creating Linear Models

Question 16:   E
Questions 17-19:   M

16

Alex works all summer cutting lawns in his neighborhood. On average, the mower uses one gallon of fuel for 2 lawns, and one quart of oil for 8 lawns. Alex charges $10 per lawn, fuel costs $3 per gallon, and oil costs $4 per quart. Which expression defines Alex's profit if L is the number of lawns Alex mows?

A) $8L$

B) $10L$

C) $10L - \left(\dfrac{3}{2} + \dfrac{4}{8} \right)$

D) $10L - \left(\dfrac{3}{2} - \dfrac{4}{8} \right)$

17

Katherine used a coupon at the grocery store for 15% off her purchase price. After paying a 6% sales tax on the discounted price, her total cost was T dollars. In terms of T, what was the cost, in dollars, of her groceries before any discount or tax was applied?

A) $0.91T$

B) $\dfrac{T}{0.91}$

C) $(1.06)(0.85)T$

D) $\dfrac{T}{(1.06)(0.85)}$

18

A soda company is expecting to produce 30,000 bottles of root beer this month. A new machine will allow the company to increase production by 10% next month and an additional 5% in the following month. How many bottles of root beer does the company expect to produce over the 3-month period?

A) (30,000)(1.15)

B) (30,000)(1.1)(1.05)

C) 30,000 + (30,000)(1.1) + (30,000)(1.1)(1.05)

D) 30,000 + (30,000)(1.1) + (30,000)(1.15)

19

An exterminator keeps cans of repellant and poison in his truck. The cans of repellant weigh 120 pounds and the cans of poison weigh 80 pounds. His truck can either carry 60 cans or a weight of 6,800 pounds. Let a be the number of cans of repellant and b be the number of cans of poison. Which of the following systems of equations describe how the truck's carrying capacity is determined?

A) $a + b \leq 60$
$120a + 80b \leq 6,800$

B) $a + 120b \leq 6,800$
$80a + b \leq 60$

C) $a - b \leq 60$
$120a - 80b \leq 6,800$

D) $a - 60 \leq b$
$120a - 6,800 \leq b$

Interpreting Linear Models

Question 20:   M

20

The growth of a nation's GDP (gross domestic product) can be modeled by the equation $y = .0613x + 20,077$, where x is the number of years since 1965 and $x < 100$. Which of the following is the best interpretation of the coefficient of x in this model?

A) The growth of GDP in a given year

B) The number of dollars spent in a given year

C) The decrease of GDP in a given year

D) The population growth of a nation in a given year

SUMMIT
EDUCATIONAL
GROUP

Miscellaneous

Questions 21-23:   E
Questions 24-32:   M
Questions 33-36:   H

21

Which of the following, when subtracted from $5x^2 + 4x + 4$, will yield $x^2 + 4x + 6$?

A) $4x^2 - 2$
B) $4x^2 + 2$
C) $4x^2 - 8x + 2$
D) $4x^2 + 8x - 2$

Category: _____

22

If $x + \dfrac{1}{2}y = 4$ what is the value of $4x + 2y$?

Category: _____

23

Which of the following values of x is NOT a solution of the inequality $3x + 3 \geq 2x - 5$?

A) −9
B) −8
C) −5
D) 3

Category: _____

24

The expression $\dfrac{6x + 30}{x + 3}$ is equivalent to which of the following?

A) $6 + 5x$
B) $\dfrac{6x}{x+3} + \dfrac{12}{x+3}$
C) $6 + \dfrac{12}{x+3}$
D) $6 - \dfrac{30}{x+3}$

Category: _____

25

Sam and Alex work at a clothing store. Last week, they sold a total of 140 shirts, with Sam selling 12 more shirts than Alex. How many shirts did Sam sell?

Category: _____

26

$$x - y = 5$$
$$6x + 3y = 21$$

Which of the following ordered pairs (x,y) satisfies the systems of equations above?

A) (0,–5)
B) (4,–1)
C) (5,0)
D) (6,1)

Category: _____

▼

Questions 27-28 refer to the following information.

A scientist uses the equation $c = 132 + 2.60d$ to describe the concentration of a dissolved mineral in a tank of water, where c is the concentration in parts per thousand and d is the depth of the water in feet.

27

What is the expression that gives the depth of the water in terms of the mineral's concentration?

A) $d = \dfrac{c - 132}{2.60}$

B) $d = \dfrac{c + 132}{2.60}$

C) $d = \dfrac{132 - c}{2.60}$

D) $d = \dfrac{2.60}{c + 132}$

Category: _____

28

At what depth will the concentration be closest to 145 parts per thousand?

A) 2 feet
B) 3 feet
C) 4 feet
D) 5 feet

Category: _____

▲

29

A mutual fund company makes 0.75% of a client's investments if they show returns on shares of Mama Maguffan's Stovetop Stuffin' and 0.45% if a client's investments show returns on shares of Dr. Dinkum's Thinkum Juice. Which of the following expressions shows how much in dollars the mutual fund will make if a client sees returns of m dollars on shares of Stuffin' and j dollars on shares of Juice?

A) $0.75m + 0.45j$
B) $0.75j + 0.45m$
C) $0.075m + 0.045j$
D) $0.0075m + 0.0045j$

Category: _____

30

The cost C of manufacturing product x is shown by the first equation below. The revenue R from selling product x is shown by the second equation below.

$$C = 12x + 270$$
$$R = 21x$$

What is the minimum number of items x that must be sold to make a profit?

A) 29
B) 30
C) 31
D) 32

Category: _____

31

Carlton goes for a jog on a 5-mile loop. He has completed 2 miles when David begins the same loop. Carlton will jog at a constant rate of 0.1 miles per minute for the remainder of his jog whereas David will jog at a constant rate of 0.2 miles per minute for the duration of his jog. How many miles will Carlton have jogged at the point when David catches up with him?

A) 3 miles
B) 4 miles
C) 5 miles
D) David will not catch Carlton

Category: _____

32

If $24 \geq 8x - 4$, what is the possible range of values for $2x - 1$?

A) $2x - 1 \geq 3.5$
B) $2x - 1 \leq 3.5$
C) $2x - 1 \geq 6$
D) $2x - 1 \leq 6$

Category: _____

 33

A certain type of vehicle consumes 1 gallon of gas for every 20 miles it is driven. In the town of Littleville, n people own this particular vehicle. On a recent Sunday, each of the n owners drove their vehicle an average of 50 miles. How many total gallons of gas were consumed by this vehicle?

A) $\dfrac{50n}{20}$

B) $50(n)(20)$

C) $\dfrac{20n}{50}$

D) $\dfrac{20}{50n}$

Category: _____

SUMMIT
EDUCATIONAL
GROUP

34

A basketball contest awards points based on the number of shots made in 30 seconds. A lay-up is worth 2 points and a 3-pointer is worth 3 points. Jason makes at least one lay-up and at least one 3-pointer, but makes more lay-ups than 3-pointers. If Jason scores a total of 15 points, how many lay-ups did he make?

Category: _____

35

x	1	2	3	4
$f(x)$	–1	2	7	14

The table above shows some values of the function f. Which of the following defines f?

A) $f(x) = 3x - 1$

B) $f(x) = -x + 3$

C) $f(x) = x^2 - 2$

D) $f(x) = -x^2 + 3$

Category: _____

SUMMIT
EDUCATIONAL
GROUP

Passport to Advanced Math

- ❏ Equations with Fractions

- ❏ Equations with Exponents

- ❏ Equations with Radicals

- ❏ Functions

- ❏ Graphs of Functions

- ❏ Quadratic Equations

- ❏ Graphs of Quadratics

- ❏ Polynomials

- ❏ Nonlinear Models

Equations with Fractions

Fraction skills are necessary throughout the Math Test. When fractions appear in algebraic expressions or equations, you should simplify by finding common denominators or clearing the fractions.

❏ **Clear Fractions** – Fractions always make things more complicated. Look to clear fractions by using one of the following strategies:

1. Multiply the equation through by a common denominator – preferably the lowest common denominator.

2. If the equation is set up as a proportion, look to cross-multiply.

3. Simplify fractions with fractions in the denominator. Remember that dividing by a fraction is the same as multiplying by the reciprocal of the fraction.

Solve for x:

$$\frac{1}{2}x + \frac{2}{3}x = \frac{7}{4}$$

Solve for x:

$$\frac{x+8}{x} = 3$$

Solve for x:

$$\frac{1}{\frac{1}{2x}} = 4$$

❏ An expression is **undefined** when a denominator is equal to 0.

PUT IT TOGETHER

1

$$3 = \frac{7}{2x+1}$$

Which of the following is a solution to the equation above?

A) $x = 2$

B) $x = \dfrac{3}{2}$

C) $x = 1$

D) $x = \dfrac{2}{3}$

2

Which of the following is equivalent to $\dfrac{\dfrac{1}{x-2}}{\dfrac{1}{x+2}}$?

Solve both algebraically and by Choosing Numbers for *x*.

A) $\dfrac{1}{2}$

B) 2

C) $1 + \dfrac{2}{x-2}$

D) $1 + \dfrac{4}{x-2}$

3

$$k = \frac{a+b}{a-b}$$

Using the equation above, which of the following expresses a in terms of b and k?

A) $a = \dfrac{b+k}{b-k}$

B) $a = \dfrac{b+k}{k-1}$

C) $a = \dfrac{b(k+1)}{b-k}$

D) $a = \dfrac{b(k+1)}{k-1}$

Equations with Exponents

Most exponent questions on the SAT deal with creating equations from exponents that have similar bases.

☐ **Exponent Rules** – Most exponent questions require you to use exponent rules to rewrite expressions. Memorize the following exponent rules.

$$x^a \cdot x^b = x^{a+b} \qquad \frac{x^a}{x^b} = x^{a-b} \qquad \left(x^a\right)^b = x^{ab}$$

$$\left(\frac{x}{y}\right)^a = \frac{x^a}{y^a} \qquad x^{-a} = \frac{1}{x^a} \qquad (xy)^a = x^a \cdot y^a$$

$$x^0 = 1 \qquad\qquad x^1 = x$$

$$2^2 \times 2^5 = \underline{\hspace{1.5cm}} \qquad \frac{x^5}{x^2} = \underline{\hspace{1.5cm}} \qquad \left(x^2\right)^3 = \underline{\hspace{2cm}}$$

$$\left(\frac{1}{3}\right)^3 = \underline{\hspace{1.5cm}} \qquad 3^{-2} = \underline{\hspace{1.5cm}} \qquad \left(5x^2y\right)^3 = \underline{\hspace{2cm}}$$

$$2^0 = \underline{\hspace{1.5cm}} \qquad 99^1 = \underline{\hspace{1.5cm}}$$

☐ **Solving for Variable in Exponent** – To solve an equation with a variable as an exponent, first make sure that each exponent has the same base. Then, set the exponents equal to each other and solve.

If $4^{(a+3)} = 16^{2a}$, what is the value of a? _____

PUT IT TOGETHER

1

$$\left(x^2\right)^{-\frac{1}{2}}\left(x^2\right)^{\frac{3}{2}}$$

Assuming x is nonzero, which of the following expressions is equivalent to the expression above?

A) x^{-4}

B) x^{-2}

C) x^2

D) x^4

2

If $\left(x^{a+b}\right)^{a-b} = x^{64}$, and $a + b = 32$, what is the value of $a - b$?

A) 1

B) 2

C) 4

D) 8

3

If $2^x \times 2^y = 2^a$ and $\dfrac{2^x}{2^y} = 2^{a-2}$, what is the value of x in terms of a?

A) $-a$

B) a

C) $a - 1$

D) $a + 1$

Equations with Radicals

❑ The root of a number is a value that, when multiplied by itself a certain number of times, gives the number. Think of roots as the inverse of exponents.

❑ A root can be expressed using a radical sign or a fractional exponent.

$$x^{\frac{a}{b}} = \sqrt[b]{x^a}$$

$4^{\left(\frac{1}{2}\right)} =$ _____ $27^{\left(\frac{1}{3}\right)} =$ _____

❑ Memorize the following rules for multiplying and dividing roots.

$$\sqrt{x} \cdot \sqrt{y} = \sqrt{xy}$$ $$\sqrt{\frac{x}{y}} = \frac{\sqrt{x}}{\sqrt{y}}$$

$\sqrt{3} \cdot \sqrt{12} =$ _____ $\sqrt{\dfrac{81}{25}} =$ _____

❑ **Solving for a Variable Underneath a Radical Sign** – To solve an equation with a variable in a radical, isolate the variable and raise both sides of the equation to the appropriate exponent.

If $4\sqrt[3]{x} = 2$, what is the value of x? _____

1. Isolate $\sqrt[3]{x}$ on one side of the equation.

2. Cube both sides of the equation.

PUT IT TOGETHER

1

If $6\sqrt{x} + 11 = 41$, what is the value of x?

A) $\sqrt{5}$

B) 5

C) 25

D) 30

2

If $\sqrt[3]{y^2 + 2} = 3$, which of the following could be a value of y?

A) -2

B) -3

C) -4

D) -5

3

If $c = 2\sqrt{2}$ and $3c = \sqrt{2x}$, what is the value of x?

A) 4

B) $12\sqrt{2}$

C) 36

D) $48\sqrt{2}$

Checkpoint Review

1

If $8(2^s) = 2^t$, what is the value of s in terms of t?

A) $\dfrac{t}{3}$

B) $3t$

C) $t + 3$

D) $t - 3$

2

$$\frac{\left(a^7 b^5 + 4a^4\right)^{\frac{1}{4}}}{4a}$$

Which of the following is equivalent to the expression above, assuming a is nonzero?

A) $\dfrac{\left(a^3 b^5\right)^{\frac{1}{4}}}{4a}$

B) $\dfrac{\left(a^3 b^5 + 4\right)^{\frac{1}{4}}}{4}$

C) $\left(a^3 b^5\right)^{\frac{1}{4}} + 4$

D) $\left(a^3 b^5 + 4\right)^{\frac{1}{4}}$

Checkpoint Review

3

If $\dfrac{x+y}{x^2-y^2}=1$, what is y in terms of x?

A) $\dfrac{x^2}{x+1}$

B) x^2-x

C) $x+1$

D) $x-1$

4

$$s=\dfrac{\left(\sqrt{\dfrac{x}{7}}\right)\left(2+\sqrt{\dfrac{x}{7}}\right)}{\left(2+\sqrt{\dfrac{x}{7}}\right)+1}\,t$$

The formula above gives s in terms of x and t. What expression gives t in terms of x and s?

A) $t=\dfrac{\left(\sqrt{\dfrac{x}{7}}\right)\left(2+\sqrt{\dfrac{x}{7}}\right)}{\left(2+\sqrt{\dfrac{x}{7}}\right)+1}\,s$

B) $t=\dfrac{\left(2+\sqrt{\dfrac{x}{7}}\right)+1}{\left(\sqrt{\dfrac{x}{7}}\right)\left(2+\sqrt{\dfrac{x}{7}}\right)}\,s$

C) $t=\sqrt{\dfrac{x}{7}}s$

D) $t=\sqrt{\dfrac{7}{x}}s$

SUMMIT
EDUCATIONAL
GROUP

Functions

Function questions generally come in two types – questions that ask you to plug numbers in and questions that ask you to plug variables or expressions in.

❑ A function is an "instruction" or "process" that will give you a single value of $f(x)$ as a result for any value of x you put in.

Important: y and $f(x)$ are interchangeable. $y = x^2$ is the same as $f(x) = x^2$.

❑ **Evaluating Functions** – To evaluate a function, simply plug that value in everywhere you see an x.

> Consider the following function: $f(x) = x^2 - 5$
>
> $f(3) =$ _____
>
> $f(a) =$ _____
>
> $f(x-1) =$ _____
>
> If $f(x) = 20$, what are two possible values for x? _____

❑ **Compound Functions** – A compound function is a combination of functions, usually written in a nested format like $f(g(x))$. This expression is described as "f of g of x."

To evaluate a compound function, first evaluate the inner function and then plug that value into the outer function.

> Given $f(x) = 4x + 1$ and $g(x) = x^2 - 2$, solve for the following:
>
> 1. $f(g(3)) =$
>
> 2. $g(f(3)) =$
>
> 3. $g(f(x+1)) =$

PUT IT TOGETHER

1

$$f(x) = x^2 + 4x$$

For the function f defined above, $f(a) = -4$. What is the value of a?

A) –4
B) –2
C) 4
D) 8

2

A function $p(x)$ has a value of 5 when $x > 0$ and a value of –5 when $x < 0$. A function q is defined as $q(x) = x^2 - 4$. What is the value of $(q(p(3))$?

A) 19
B) 20
C) 21
D) 24

3

If $g(x) = 2x - 10$, which of the following must be equal to $g(g(x))$?

A) $4x^2 - 40x + 100$
B) $4x^2 + 100$
C) $4x^2 - 100$
D) $4x - 30$

Graphs of Functions

Not only do you need to know how to evaluate functions algebraically, you also need to know how to use the graph of a function to find the value of y or $f(x)$ – remember they are the same – when given the value of x (or vice-versa).

❑ Remember: y and $f(x)$ are the same. $f(x)$ is the y-coordinate of function f for a value x.

$f(2)$, for example, is the y-coordinate of the point on the graph of f where $x = 2$.

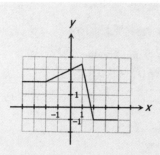

The graph of $y = f(x)$ is shown above.

$f(0) = \underline{\hspace{1cm}}$

$f(-2) = \underline{\hspace{1cm}}$

For how many values of x does $f(x) = 2.5$? $\underline{\hspace{2cm}}$

❑ **Function Transformation** – Occasionally, you will be asked to identify how changes to a function affect the graph of the function. You should memorize the following rules. Also, note that you can solve some graph transformation questions by plugging in sets of coordinates.

$f(x) + n$ shifts the graph UP by n units.

$f(x) - n$ shifts the graph DOWN by n units.

$f(x + n)$ shifts the graph to the LEFT by n units.

$f(x - n)$ shifts the graph to the RIGHT by n units.

$-f(x)$ reflects the graph over the x-axis.

$f(-x)$ reflects the graph over the y-axis.

PUT IT TOGETHER

1

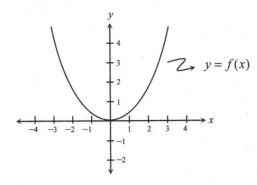

Draw a line at $y = 3$ to help visualize.

The function $y = f(x)$ is graphed above. For how many values of x does $f(x) = 3$?

A) 3
B) 2
C) 1
D) 0

2

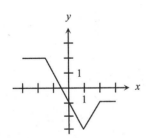

The graph of $y = g(x)$ is shown above. If $g(a) = -2$, which of the following is a possible value of a?

A) −2.5
B) −1
C) 0.5
D) 2.5

SUMMIT
EDUCATIONAL
GROUP

3

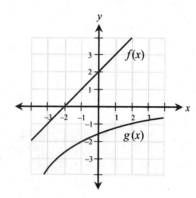

The graphs of $f(x)$ and $g(x)$ are shown in the xy-plane above. What is the value of $g(f(0))$?

A) −2.5

B) −1.5

C) −1

D) 0

Solve like you would solve a compound function question: evaluate the inner function and then plug that value into the other function.

4

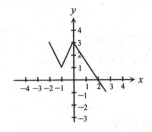

The graph of $y = f(x)$ is shown above. Which of the following could be the graph of $f(x-1)+1$?

A)

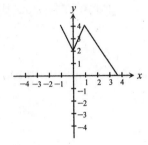

B)

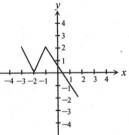

C)

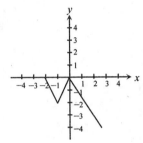

D)

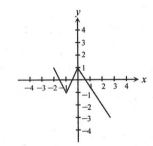

Quadratic Equations

Most questions in this category will test your ability to solve quadratic equations by factoring or by using the quadratic formula. Some questions will ask you to determine the types of solutions.

❏ A quadratic equation has a squared term as the term with the highest power. For example, $x^2 - 2x + 17 = 0$ is a quadratic equation.

The solutions to a quadratic equation are called **solutions**, **roots**, or **zeros**. Graphically, the solutions to a quadratic equation are where the graph intercepts the x-axis (the **x-intercepts**), where the y value is zero.

❏ **Factoring and Solving Quadratics** – Solve quadratic equations by following four simple steps:

1. Set the equation equal to 0.

2. Factor the equation.

3. Set each factor equal to 0.

4. Solve each of the resulting equations.

> Solve for x: $x^2 - 5x = -6$
>
> 1. _____
>
> 2. _____
>
> 3. _____
>
> 4. _____

❑ Sometimes, you'll be able to use the common quadratics covered in the Algebraic Expressions module to simplify the factoring step.

$(a + b)^2 =$ $(a + b)(a + b) = a^2 + ab + ba + b^2$ $= a^2 + 2ab + b^2$

$(a - b)^2 =$ $(a - b)(a - b) = a^2 - ab - ba + (-b)^2$ $= a^2 - 2ab + b^2$

$(a + b)(a - b) =$ $a^2 - ab + ba - b^2$ $= a^2 - b^2$

❑ **Quadratic Formula** – If a quadratic equation cannot be easily factored, use the quadratic formula.

For an equation $ax^2 + bx + c = 0$, $x = \dfrac{-b \pm \sqrt{b^2 - 4ac}}{2a}$

Solve: $2x^2 + 5x + 1 = 0$

❑ **The Discriminant** – The discriminant is that part of the quadratic formula under the radical sign: $b^2 - 4ac$. You can use it to help you determine the types of solutions or roots the quadratic equation has.

$b^2 - 4ac > 0$ 2 real roots

$b^2 - 4ac = 0$ 1 real, rational root

$b^2 - 4ac < 0$ 2 complex roots

$b^2 - 4ac$ is positive and a perfect square   2 real, rational roots

$b^2 - 4ac$ is positive and not a perfect square   2 real, irrational roots

Explain why the above determinations can be made from examining the discriminant.

PUT IT TOGETHER

1

If $a^2 + 5a + 14 = (a-2)(a+7) + k$, then $k =$

A) -28
B) -14
C) 14
D) 28

2

A quadratic equation has the solutions $y = 3$ and $y = -4$. Which of the following could be the equation for the quadratic?

A) $y = 12 - y^2$
B) $y = y^2 - 12$
C) $y = 1 - y^2$
D) $y = y^2 - 1$

3

$$g(x) = \frac{1}{4(x-5)^2 - 1}$$

For what value of x is function g undefined?

A) $5\frac{1}{4}$
B) 5
C) $4\frac{1}{2}$
D) 1

4

$$0 = m^2 + 2m - 7$$

Based on the equation shown above, which of the following are the solutions for m?

A) $-1 \pm 2\sqrt{2}$

B) $1 \pm 2\sqrt{2}$

C) -1 ± 4

D) 1 ± 4

5

$$x^2 + 3(x - 4) = 0$$

Which of the following best describes the set of solutions for the quadratic equation shown above?

A) Two distinct, real solutions

B) Two distinct, imaginary solutions

C) One real solution

D) No solutions

Graphs of Quadratics

The SAT requires that you understand and can move fluidly among the different forms of quadratic functions: Standard form, Intercept form, and Vertex form. The intercept and vertex forms are useful for graphing quadratic functions. The graph of a quadratic equation is called a parabola.

❑ **Standard form:** $y = ax^2 + bx + c$

❑ **Intercept form:** $y = a(x - p)(x - q)$

> In intercept form, p and q are the x-intercepts, where $f(x) = 0$.
>
> Convert a quadratic equation from standard form to intercept form by factoring.

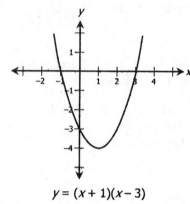

$$y = (x + 1)(x - 3)$$

x-intercepts $= -1$ and 3

❑ **Vertex form:** $y = a(x - h)^2 + k$

> In vertex form, (h, k) are the coordinates of the vertex of the parabola.

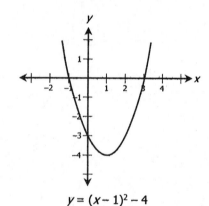

$$y = (x - 1)^2 - 4$$

vertex: $(1, -4)$

❏ If a quadratic equation is in standard form, you can convert it to vertex form by "completing the square."

For an expression $x^2 + bx$, rewrite as $\left(x + \dfrac{b}{2} \right)^2$, then FOIL and rebalance the equation.

$y = 2x^2 + 12x - 8$

Step 1: Bring the "loose" term (8) over to the left side.

_____

Step 2: Factor out the coefficient on the squared term from both terms on the right.

_____

Step 3: For your quadratic expression of the form $x^2 + bx$, write a new expression of the form $\left(x + \dfrac{b}{2} \right)^2$.

Note that these two expressions are <u>not</u> equal. $\left(x + \dfrac{b}{2} \right)^2 = x^2 + bx + \dfrac{b^2}{4}$.

The new expression is exactly $\dfrac{b^2}{4}$ more than the original. To compensate for this, you must add the product of $\dfrac{b^2}{4}$ and its coefficient to the left side. This keeps the equation balanced.

_____

Step 4: Rewrite the equation in vertex form.

_____

Step 5: What are the coordinates of the parabola's vertex?

_____

PUT IT TOGETHER

$$y = 2x(x+1) - 6(x+1)$$

Which of the following is the graph in the *xy*-plane of the equation shown above?

> Which graph has *x*-intercepts that are the zeros of the equation?

A)

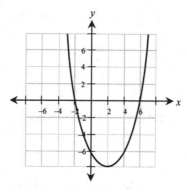

B)

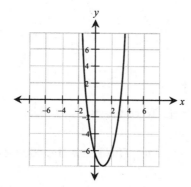

C)

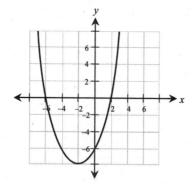

D)

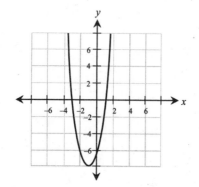

2

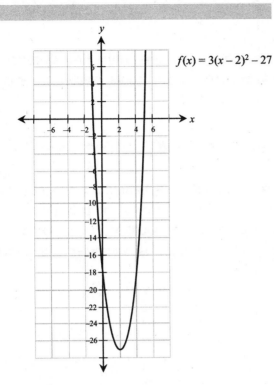

$f(x) = 3(x-2)^2 - 27$

The graph of $y = f(x)$ in the xy-plane is a parabola with vertex at $(2, -27)$, as shown above. Which of the following is an equivalent form of the equation which shows the x-intercepts of the parabola as constants?

A) $f(x) = 3(x-5)(x-(-1))$

B) $f(x) = 3(x-11)^2$

C) $f(x) = (3x-9)(x-2)$

D) $f(x) = 3x^2 - 12x - 15$

> The x-intercepts of a parabola appear as constants when a quadratic equation is written in intercept form.

3

$$f(x) = 2(x-1)(x+3)$$

The graph of the equation above is a parabola in the xy-plane. In which of the following equivalent forms of the function f do the xy-coordinates of the vertex of the parabola appear as constants or coefficients?

A) $f(x) = 2x^2 + 4x - 6$

B) $f(x) = 2(x^2 + 2x - 3)$

C) $f(x) = 2(x+2)^2 - 2$

D) $f(x) = 2(x+1)^2 - 8$

Polynomials

Polynomial questions are some of the more challenging questions on the SAT. Questions typically involve a solid grasp of the connection between factors, roots, solutions, zeros, and x-intercepts.

❑ A polynomial is the sum of terms with variables raised to whole-number exponents.

❑ A **solution** to a polynomial equation is also a **root** of the equation, a **zero** of the function, and an **x-intercept**. Any of these can be used to find a factor of the polynomial. In other words, if you know one of these for a polynomial equation, you can find the others. You should be able to move fluidly among roots, zeros, x-intercepts, and factors.

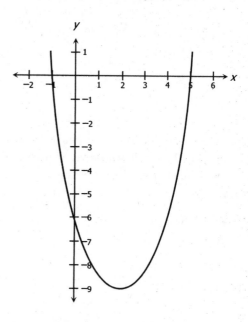

$f(x) = x^2 - 4x - 5$

Solve: $x^2 - 4x - 5 = 0$

$(x - 5)(x + 1) = 0$

$(x - 5)$ and $(x + 1)$ are factors of $f(x)$.

Set each factor equal to 0 to see that $x = 5$ and $x = -1$ are solutions to the equation.

$x = 5$ and $x = -1$ are the zeros of $f(x)$. A zero is the value of x (the input) that produces an output of 0.

In other words, $f(5)$ and $f(-1)$ both equal 0.

Since $x = 5$ and $x = -1$ are zeros of $f(x)$, these are the x-intercepts of the graph of $f(x)$.

One solution to the equation $P(x) = 0$, where P is a polynomial function, is $x = 6$.
What are the coordinates of one of the x-intercepts of $P(x)$?
What is one factor of $P(x)$?

If $P(x) = (x - 3)(x + 1)(x^2)$, what are the zeros of $P(x)$?

What are the x-intercepts?

If $(x + 3)$ is a factor of a polynomial $P(x)$, what is the value of P when $x = -3$?

If a polynomial $P(x)$ has zeros at 1, 3, and −1, what might the equation of $P(x)$ be?

❑ Find the solutions of a polynomial by setting the polynomial equal to zero and factoring. Once in factored form, set each factor equal to zero to find the solutions. Consider group factoring if the usual factoring isn't working.

Solve:

$y = 2x^3 + 10x^2 + 12x$

Solve:

$y = x^3 + 2x^2 + 8x + 16$

❑ **Dividing polynomials** – If a polynomial divides evenly into another polynomial, then both the divisor and the quotient are factors of the polynomial. If there is a remainder, then neither is a factor.

If $P(x)$ divided by $x - 2$ equals $x^2 + 2x - 8$, what are the factors of $P(x)$?

What are the zeros of $P(x)$?

❑ **Polynomial Long Division** – To divide a polynomial by a binomial factor, set up a long division problem with the polynomial written in descending powers of x.

$$
\begin{array}{r}
2x^2 + x - 9 \\
x+4{\overline{\smash{\big)}\,2x^3 + 9x^2 - 5x - 36}} \\
\underline{2x^3 + 8x^2} \\
x^2 - 5x \\
\underline{x^2 + 4x} \\
-9x - 36 \\
\underline{-9x - 36} \\
0
\end{array}
$$

PUT IT TOGETHER

1

The function f is defined by a polynomial. If $(-3,0)$, $(0,-2)$, and $(2,4)$ are points on the graph of the function, which of the following must be a factor of $f(x)$?

A) $x + 3$
B) $x + 2$
C) $x - 2$
D) $x - 4$

2

$$x^3 - 19x + 30$$

Which of the following is a factor of the polynomial shown above?

A) $(x - 15)$
B) $(x - 5)$
C) $(x - 2)$
D) $(x + 3)$

3

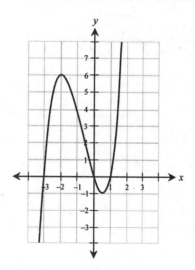

Which of the following could represent the graph shown in the xy-plane above?

A) $y = x^3 + 2x^2 - 3x$
B) $y = x^3 - 2x^2 - 3x$
C) $y = x^3 + 5x^2 - 6x + 3$
D) $y = x^3 - 6x^2 + 5x - 3$

4

Function f is a polynomial with a double zero at -1 and a double zero at 0. Which of the following could be the equation of the polynomial?

A) $f(x) = x^2 - 2x + 1$

B) $f(x) = x^2 + 2x + 1$

C) $f(x) = x^4 - 2x^3 + x^2$

D) $f(x) = x^4 + 2x^3 + x^2$

> If a polynomial has two of the same factor, it has a double zero at the value of x for which the factor equals zero.

5

The remainder when polynomial $f(x)$ is divided by $x + 1$ is 3. Which of the following must be true about $f(x)$?

A) $f(1) = 3$

B) $f(-1) = 3$

C) $(x + 4)$ is a factor of $f(x)$

D) $(x - 2)$ is a factor of $f(x)$

> Remainder Theorem:
> When polynomial $f(x)$ is divided by $x - c$, the remainder is equal to $f(c)$.

SUMMIT
EDUCATIONAL
GROUP

Nonlinear Models

Nonlinear model questions require that you make connections between a real-world situation and the algebraic equation that models that situation. Common scenarios deal with exponential growth and decay (e.g., compound interest, population growth, half-lives of radioactive material) and projectile motion (e.g., an arrow being shot into the air).

❑ **Exponential Relationship** – An exponential relationship is one in which the rate of change increases over time (exponential growth) or decreases over time (exponential decay).

Algebraically, an exponential relationship is expressed as $y = ab^x$.

In this form, for a typical SAT question, a is the initial value, b is the amount of change per unit of time, and x is the amount of time.

The graph to the right shows the population growth of a swarm of locusts. The population grows by 30% per week.
The population, p, at week w is given by the function $p = 10{,}000 \times (1.3)^w$.

What does 10,000 represent in the equation?

What does 1.3 represent in the equation?

What will the population be in week 4?

What will the population be in week 10?

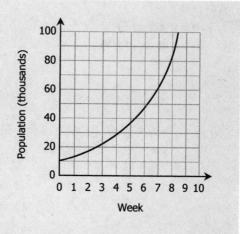

❑ **Quadratic Relationship** – A quadratic relationship first increases quickly, slows, and then decreases quickly, or vice versa.

This is expressed algebraically as $y = ax^2 + bx + c$.

In this form, for a typical SAT question, c is the initial value and x is the amount of time.

The graph to the right shows the height of a ball after it is thrown, which is defined by the function $h(t) = -16t^2 + 30t + 4$, where h is the height of the ball in feet and t is the time in seconds after the ball is thrown.

What is the meaning of 4 in the equation?

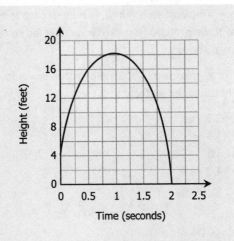

After how many seconds does the ball descend back down to its original height?

What is the ball's maximum height?

PUT IT TOGETHER

1

$$h(t) = -3.9t^2 + 16t$$

If an astronaut on the surface of Mars were to throw a stone vertically upward at 16 meters per second, the stone's increase in height h, in meters, t seconds after it was thrown, could be approximated by the equation shown above.

After approximately how many seconds would the stone fall back to the surface?

A) 2.5
B) 3.0
C) 3.5
D) 4.0

Questions 2-3 refer to the following information.

Research Team A grows bacteria in a Petri dish. There are initially 200 bacteria in the dish and the number of bacteria increases 4% each hour. The researchers use the expression $200(r)^t$ to estimate the number of bacteria present after t hours.

2

What is the value of r in the expression?

A) 0.04
B) 0.96
C) 1.04
D) 4.00

3

Research Team B grows the same bacteria in an identical Petri dish but they use an antibacterial agent to slow the growth rate to 1.5% per hour. If Team B also starts with 200 bacteria, how many more bacteria will be in Team A's Petri dish than Team B's Petri dish after 24 hours? (Round to the nearest whole number.)

A) 120
B) 151
C) 227
D) 5,212

Passport to Advanced Math Summary

❏ **Equations with Fractions** – Fractions always make things more complicated. Look to clear fractions by using one of the following strategies:

1. Multiply the equation through by a common denominator – preferably the lowest common denominator.

2. If the equation is set up as a proportion, look to cross-multiply.

3. Simplify fractions with fractions in the denominator. Remember that dividing by a fraction is the same as multiplying by the reciprocal of the fraction.

❏ An expression is **undefined** when a denominator is equal to 0.

❏ **Solving for Variable in Exponent** – To solve an equation with a variable as an exponent, first make sure that each exponent has the same base. Then set the exponents equal to each other and solve.

❏ **Solving for a Variable Underneath a Radical Sign** – To solve an equation with a variable in a radical, isolate the variable and raise both sides of the equation to the appropriate exponent.

❏ **Evaluating Functions** – To evaluate a function, simply plug that value in everywhere you see an x.

❏ **Compound Functions** – A compound function is a combination of functions, usually written in a nested format like $f(g(x))$. This is described as "f of g of x." To evaluate a compound function, first evaluate the inner function and then plug that value into the outer function.

❏ Remember: y and $f(x)$ are the same. $f(x)$ is the y-coordinate of function f for a value x.

❏ **Factoring and Solving Quadratics** – Solve quadratic equations by following four simple steps:

1. Set the equation equal to 0.

2. Factor the equation.

3. Set each factor equal to 0.

4. Solve each of the resulting equations.

❏ **The Discriminant** – The discriminant is the part of the quadratic formula under the radical sign: $b^2 - 4ac$. You can use it to help you determine the types of solutions or roots the quadratic equation has.

❏ **Completing the Square** – If a quadratic equation is in standard form, you can convert it to vertex form by "completing the square."

For an expression $x^2 + bx$, rewrite as $\left(x + \dfrac{b}{2}\right)^2$, then FOIL and rebalance the equation.

❏ **Polynomial Solutions** – A **solution** to a polynomial equation is also a **root** of the equation, a **zero** of the function, and an **x-intercept**. Any of these can be used to find a factor of the polynomial.
Find the solutions of a polynomial by setting the polynomial equal to zero and factoring. Once in factored form, set each factor equal to zero to find the solutions. Consider group factoring if the usual factoring isn't working.

❏ **Dividing polynomials** – If a polynomial divides evenly into another polynomial, then both the divisor and the quotient are factors of the polynomial. If there is a remainder, then neither is a factor.

❏ **Exponential Relationship** – An exponential relationship is one in which the rate of change increases over time (exponential growth) or decreases over time (exponential decay). Algebraically, an exponential relationship is expressed as $y = ab^x$.

In this form, for a typical SAT question, a is the initial value, b is the amount of change per unit of time, and x is the amount of time.

❏ **Quadratic Relationship** – A quadratic relationship first increases quickly, slows, and then decreases quickly, or vice versa. This is expressed algebraically as $y = ax^2 + bx + c$.

In this form, for a typical SAT question, c is the initial value and x is the amount of time.

Passport to Advanced Math Practice

Equations with Fractions

Question 1:   E
Questions 2-3:   M

1

If $\dfrac{12x}{y} = 2$, what is the value of $\dfrac{y}{x}$?

A) 2
B) 4
C) 6
D) 7

 2

$$\dfrac{2}{(x+2)^2 - 6(x+2) + 9}$$

For what value of x is the above expression undefined?

 3

If j is an integer, and $\dfrac{3j-2}{j} = 3j - 2$, which of the following best describes the solution set to the equation shown above?

A) The equation has exactly one solution, $j = 1$.
B) The equation has exactly one solution, $j = 0$.
C) The equation has no solutions.
D) The equation has infinitely many solutions.

Equations with Exponents

Questions 4-5:   E
Question 6:   M

 4

If $x^3 = a$ and $x^7 = b$, which of the following must be equal to x^8?

A) $a^2 b^2$
B) $\dfrac{b^2}{a^2}$
C) ab^2
D) $2(b - a)$

5

$6m^3 n^2$ is the product of $3mn$ and

A) $2m^2 n^2$
B) $2m^3 n^2$
C) $2m^2 n$
D) $2mn^2$

 6

If $3^{n+3} = 9^{2n}$, then $n =$

Radical Equations

Question 7:   E
Question 8:   M

7

$$\left(\sqrt{\frac{1}{3}+\frac{1}{6}}\right)\left(\sqrt{2}\right)=$$

A) $\dfrac{\sqrt{3}}{2}$

B) 1

C) $\dfrac{3}{2}$

D) $\dfrac{3\sqrt{2}}{2}$

8

If $\sqrt[3]{3x^2}=3$, what is the value of $|x|$?

Functions

Question 9:   E
Questions 10-11:   M

9

If $f(x)=x^2-kx-8$, and $f(2)=0$, what is the value of k?

A) –4

B) –2

C) 0

D) 2

10

$$f(x)=\frac{ax^2+12}{6-x}$$

For the function f defined above, a is constant and $f(4)=10$. What is the value of $f(-4)$?

A) $\dfrac{-10}{3}$

B) 2

C) $\dfrac{9}{2}$

D) 10

11

Let $f(x)=ax^2+bx+c$ for all real numbers x. If $f(0)=2$ and $f(1)=1$, then $a+b=$

A) –2

B) –1

C) 1

D) 2

Graphing Functions

Questions 12-13:   E
Question 14:   M

12

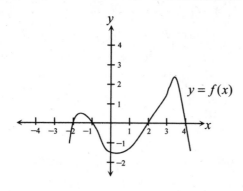

For the portion of the graph of $f(x)$ shown above, for what values of x is $f(x) > 0$?

A) $-2 < x < -1$ only

B) $0 < x < 2$ only

C) $2 < x < 4$ only

D) $-2 < x < -1$ and $2 < x < 4$

13

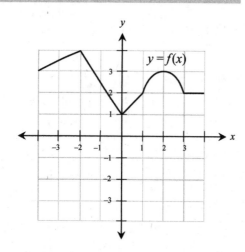

The figure above shows the complete graph of the function f. For what value of x is the value of $f(x)$ at its maximum?

A) -2

B) 0

C) 4

D) 5

14

$$f(x) - 1 = g(x+1) - 1$$

Consider the functions above. Which of the following best describes how to transform the graph of function g into the graph of function f?

A) Move the graph of function g down 1 and to the left 1.

B) Move the graph of function g down 1 and to the right 1.

C) Move the graph of function g to the left 1.

D) Move the graph of function g to the right 1.

Quadratic Equations

Question 15:   E
Question 16:   M

15

What is the product of all values that satisfy $x^2 - 25 = 0$?

A) -25

B) -10

C) 10

D) 25

16

If $(ax - 3)(bx + 6) = 24x^2 + cx - 18$ for all values of x, and $a + b = 10$, what are two possible values for c?

A) 2 and 12

B) 6 and 24

C) 10 and 30

D) 16 and 30

Graphs of Quadratics

Question 17:   M

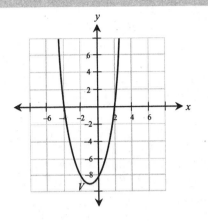

For the graph in the xy-plane shown above, which of the following equations correctly describes the graph and contains the coordinates of the vertex V as constants?

A) $f(x) = (x-2)(x+4)$

B) $f(x) = (x+2)(x-4)$

C) $f(x) = x(x+2)-8$

D) $f(x) = (x-(-1))^2 - 9$

Polynomials

Question 18:   H

For a polynomial $q(x)$, the value of $q(5)$ is 12. Which of the following statements must be true about $q(x)$?

A) The remainder when $q(x)$ is divided by $x-5$ is 12.

B) $x + 17$ is a factor of $q(x)$.

C) $x - 12$ is a factor of $q(x)$.

D) $x + 12$ is a factor of $q(x)$.

Nonlinear Models

Question 19:   M

A bicycle store wishes to sell its remaining bikes from last year's model. As of today, the full price is $750 but for each successive week, the price will drop by 10% from the previous week's price. Which of the following functions P models the price t weeks from now?

A) $P(t) = 750(.9)^t$

B) $P(t) = 750(.1)^t$

C) $P(t) = 750 - 750(.9t)$

D) $P(t) = 750 - 750(.1t)$

SUMMIT
EDUCATIONAL
GROUP

Miscellaneous

Questions 20-24:   E
Questions 25-29:   M
Questions 30-32:   H

20

$$\frac{\left(a-\frac{7}{2}\right)^2-4}{3}=15$$

Which of the following is the positive solution to the equation above?

A) $\frac{21}{4}$

B) 7

C) 10

D) $\frac{21}{2}$

Category: _____

21

If $y=\frac{1}{2}x$, which of the following is equivalent to y^3+y?

A) $\frac{1}{4}x^3+x$

B) $\frac{1}{8}x^3+\frac{1}{2}x$

C) $\frac{1}{16}x^3+\frac{1}{4}x$

D) $\frac{1}{32}x^3+\frac{1}{8}x$

Category: _____

22

If $d<0$ and $d^4-16=0$, what is the value of d?

A) −4

B) −2

C) 2

D) 4

Category: _____

23

Which of the following shows the graph of a function f such that $f(x)\neq0$ for the portion shown?

A)

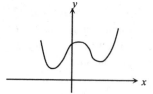

B)

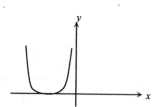

C)

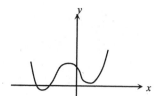

D)

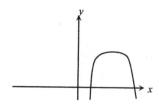

Category: _____

24

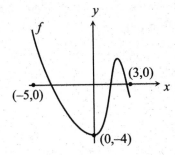

The graph of $y = f(x)$ is shown above. Assuming that $-5 \le x \le 3$, for how many values of x does $f(x) = -3$?

A) None
B) One
C) Two
D) Three

Category: _____

 25

Which of the following equations has a graph in the xy-plane for which y could be less than 0?

A) $y = x^3$
B) $y = x^2$
C) $y = x^{-2}$
D) $y = (-x)^2$

Category: _____

26

$$(bc)^a - d = 0$$

If $d = 16$, $a > b > c > 0$, and a, b, and c are all integers, what is the value of b?

A) 1
B) 2
C) 3
D) 4

Category: _____

 27

If $(x^a)(x^b) = x^7$ and $\dfrac{x^a}{x^b} = x^3$, what is the value of b?

A) 2
B) 3
C) 5
D) 7

Category: _____

28

Which of the following functions never has a value that is less than –2?

A) $f(x) = |x| - 3$

B) $f(x) = -x^2 + 3$

C) $f(x) = (x+2)(x-2)$

D) $f(x) = x^2 + 2x + 1$

Category: _____

 29

If $x > 0$, then $\left(y\sqrt{x}\right)^2 \div 5x^2 y =$

A) $5xy$

B) $\dfrac{5}{x}$

C) $\dfrac{y}{5x}$

D) $\dfrac{1}{5x}$

Category: _____

30

The thickness of the base of a hurricane barrier is a function of its height. If h represents the height of the hurricane barrier in feet and $T(h)$ represents the thickness of the base of the hurricane barrier in yards, then

$T(h) = \dfrac{1}{9}(h^2 - 2h + 9)$. What is the height, in feet, of the base of a hurricane barrier that is 12 yards thick?

A) 11
B) 13
C) 33
D) 189

Category: _____

31

How much more than p is the expression $\dfrac{5p-1}{6} + \dfrac{p+5}{6}$?

Category: _____

32

If $p^2 + q^2 = -2pq$, which of the following gives the value of p for all values of q?

A) -1
B) 0
C) $-q$
D) q

Category: _____

SUMMIT
EDUCATIONAL
GROUP

Additional Topics in Math

- ❏ Reference Information

- ❏ Angles

- ❏ Triangles

- ❏ Circles

- ❏ Volume

- ❏ Trigonometry

- ❏ Complex Numbers

Reference Information

❑ Do your best to memorize the formulas and rules given below, but remember that they are at the beginning of every SAT Math section.

REFERENCE

     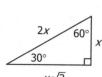

$A = \pi r^2$

$c = 2\pi r$

$A = lw$

$A = \frac{1}{2}bh$

$c^2 = a^2 + b^2$

Special Right Triangles

$V = lwh$

$V = \pi r^2 h$

$V = \frac{4}{3}\pi r^3$

$V = \frac{1}{3}\pi r^2 h$

$V = \frac{1}{3}lwh$

The number of degrees of arc in a circle is 360.
The number of radians of arc in a circle is 2π.
The sum of the measures in degrees of the angles of a triangle is 180.

Angles

Angle questions usually require you to use a combination of several angle rules in order to find the measure of an unknown angle or angles. Calculate and label missing angles, and if a figure is not drawn, draw one. Calculations often involve algebra.

❑ Memorize the following properties of angles.

Right Angle:

$x =$ _____

Circle:

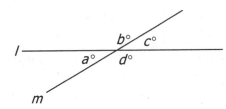

$a + b + c + d =$ _____

Vertical Angles:

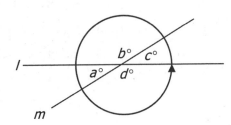

$a =$ _____ ; $b =$ _____

Triangle:

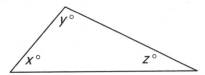

$x + y + z =$ _____

Quadrilateral:

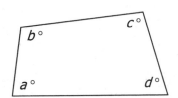

$a + b + c + d =$ _____

❑ The sum of the interior angles of any polygon = $(n-2) \times 180°$, where n is the number of sides. Note that you can also divide a polygon into triangles to determine the sum of the interior angles.

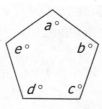

$a + b + c + d + e = $ _____

If all angles are equal, $a = $ _____

❑ When a line crosses through two parallel lines, it creates several sets of equal angles and supplementary angles. The obtuse angles are equal and the acute angles are equal. The sum of an obtuse angle and an acute angle is 180°.

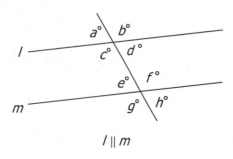

$l \parallel m$

$a = d$ **vertical angles**

$d = e$ **alternate interior angles**

$a = e$ **corresponding angles**

$a = h$ **alternate exterior angles**

$a = d = e = h$

$b = c = f = g$

❑ When a problem contains parallel lines, identify and label all equal angles. Calculate any remaining angles where possible. If a figure is not drawn, draw one!

If $l \parallel m$, and one angle is given as shown, label the unmarked angles in the figure below.

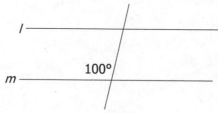

❑ A line tangent to a circle is perpendicular to the radius at the point where the line meets the circle.

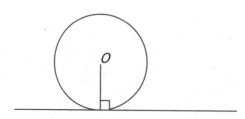

PUT IT TOGETHER

1

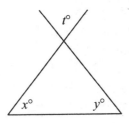

In the figure above, what is the value of t in terms of x and y?

A) $180 - x - y$
B) $180 + x - y$
C) $180 - x + y$
D) $360 - 2x - 2y$

2

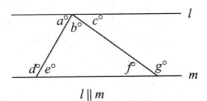

$l \parallel m$

In the figure above, $a + c$ equals which of the following?

I. $e + f$
II. $180 - b$
III. $360 - g - d$

A) I only
B) I and II
C) II and III
D) I, II, and III

3

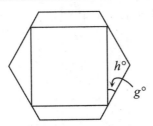

A rectangle is inscribed inside of a regular hexagon, as shown above. What is the value of g?

A) 30
B) 35
C) 40
D) 45

Triangles

The most common type of SAT triangle question will require you to recognize and solve similar triangles, but you'll also have to know other properties of triangles.

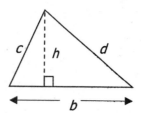

Area = _____

Perimeter = _____

- [ ] In an **isosceles** triangle, two sides are equal, and the two angles opposite those sides are equal.

  The straight line that bisects the vertex angle of an isosceles triangle is the perpendicular bisector of the base.

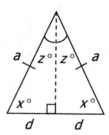

- [ ] The hypotenuse is the longest side of a right triangle. It is opposite the right angle.

  The two non-right angles have a sum of 90°.

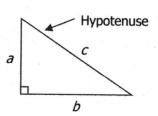

- [ ] **Pythagorean Theorem**: $a^2 + b^2 = c^2$

Use the Pythagorean Theorem to find the length of the missing leg of each right triangle.

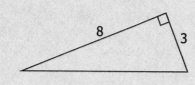

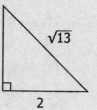

- [ ] Special right triangle rules are provided in the introduction to the SAT Math Test.

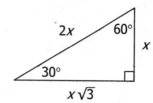

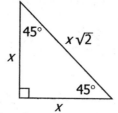

❑ **Similar triangles** have corresponding angles that are equal and corresponding sides that are proportional. Similar triangles have the same shape but not necessarily the same size. Solve similar triangle questions by setting up a proportion of side lengths.

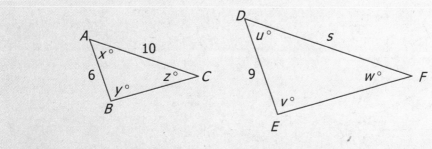

If triangles *ABC* and *DEF* are similar, what proportion will allow you to find the value of *s* ?

_____

What is the value of *s*? _____

What is true about the values of *x* and *u*? *y* and *v*? *z* and *w*? _____

❑ Before you can solve similar triangles, you first need to recognize when you're faced with similar triangles. Both of the following scenarios create similar triangles:

Parallel line inside a triangle:

If $\overline{AB}$ is parallel to $\overline{DE}$, and

$\overline{DE}$ = *x*, what is the length of

$\overline{AB}$ in terms of *x*? _____

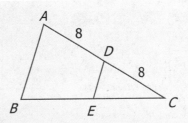

Equal angles created by intersecting lines, parallel lines, or isosceles triangles:

In the figure to the right, $\overline{AB}$ ∥$\overline{DE}$.
Are triangles *ABC* and *DEC* similar?
Why or why not?

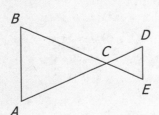

_____

_____

_____

PUT IT TOGETHER

  1

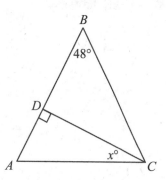

In the figure above, triangle *ABC* is isosceles with
AB = *BC*. $\overline{CD}$ is perpendicular to $\overline{AB}$. What is the value
of *x*?

2

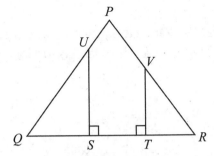

Note: Figure not drawn to scale.

In triangle PQR above, $PQ = PR$ and $QS = 36$. If $US = 45$ and $VT = 35$, what is the length of $\overline{TR}$?

A) 44

B) $\dfrac{175}{4}$

C) $\dfrac{144}{5}$

D) 28

Circles

There are typically two types of circle questions on the SAT. One category asks you manipulate and/or interpret equations of circles in the coordinate plane. The other category asks you about area and arc length of circles.

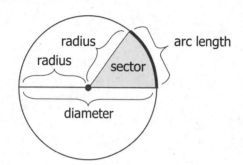

Area = _____

Circumference = _____

Diameter = _____

$\pi \approx$ _____

Complete the table below.

Area	Circumference	Radius	Diameter
16π			
	10π		
		$\sqrt{2}$	
			5

❑ The area of a sector is a fraction of the area of the circle. Similarly, an arc length is a fraction of the circumference. In both cases, the fraction is determined by the central angle.

Area of Sector $AOB = \dfrac{x}{360}\left(\pi r^2\right)$

Length of Arc $AB = \dfrac{x}{360}\left(2\pi r\right)$

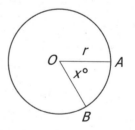

In the figure, the circle with center O has a radius of 6.

What is the length of arc AB? _____

What is the area of sector AOB? _____

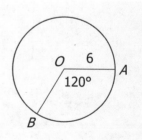

❑ **Center-Radius Equation of a Circle: $(x-h)^2 + (y-k)^2 = r^2$**

In this form, (h, k) is the center and r is the radius.

A circle centered at the origin has the equation $x^2 + y^2 = r^2$.

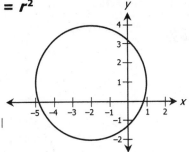

> What is the equation of a circle with a radius of 4 and a center at point (0,3)?
>
> _____

$$(x+2)^2 + (y-1)^2 = 9$$

center: $(-2,1)$

radius: 3

❑ Not all circle equations are given in "center-radius" form. In those cases, you'll have to "Complete the Square" to get the equation into "center-radius" form.

> Complete the Square to find the center and radius for the circle defined by the following equation: $x^2 + y^2 - 2x + 6y - 26 = 0$
>
> Center: _____
>
> Radius: _____

PUT IT TOGETHER

1

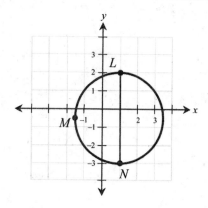

In the *xy*-plane above, $\overline{LN}$ is a diameter. What is the length of arc $\overset{\frown}{LMN}$?

A) 2.5π
B) 3.125π
C) 5π
D) 6.25π

2

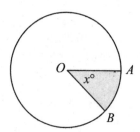

Note: Figure not drawn to scale.

The circle above has center *O* and circumference 16π. If the value of *x* is between 30 and 40, which of the following is a possible area of sector *AOB*?

A) 8π
B) 7π
C) 5π
D) 4π

3

$$(x-2)^2 + (y+3)^2 = 49$$

The equation above represents a circle in the *xy*-plane. Which of the following coordinates represent a point on the circumference of the circle?

A) (5,3)

B) (2,5)

C) (−2,−4)

D) (−5,−3)

Volume

The test instructions for the Math Test include virtually all of the important geometry formulas, including those for volume. Most volume questions on the test involve cylinders and cones, such as calculating the volume of a storage silo.

❑ The following volume formulas are provided in the test instructions. Memorizing them will save you the time of looking back during the test.

$$V = lwh \qquad V = \pi r^2 h \qquad V = \frac{4}{3}\pi r^3 \qquad V = \frac{1}{3}\pi r^2 h \qquad V = \frac{1}{3} lwh$$

❑ Set up volume questions using the correct formula. Plug in the values you know and solve the resulting algebraic equation for what you don't know.

Make sure you answer the question that is being asked. For example, if the question is asking for diameter and you've found the radius, you'll have to double it.

❑ Volume questions may require you to use the actual value of π rather than the symbol, π. Remember that π is approximately equal to 3.14.

> 23π cubic meters = _____ cubic meters

PUT IT TOGETHER

1

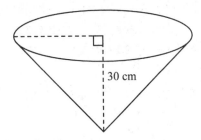

A container in the shape of the right circular cone above has a volume of $7{,}290\pi$ cm^3. What is the diameter, in centimeters, of the base of the cone?

2

A glass décor manufacturer produces right cylindrical vases with internal diameter of 12 cm and a height of 25 cm. If the manufacturer designs a smaller right cylindrical vase that holds 30% as much water and has a height of 30 cm, what is the internal diameter, in centimeters, of the smaller vase?

A) 36
B) 18
C) 6
D) 3

Trigonometry

Trigonometry is tested lightly on the SAT. Typical questions will ask you to solve right triangles by using trig ratios (think SOHCAHTOA), trig identities, and the relationship of the sine and cosine of complementary angles. You'll also need to convert between radians and degrees.

❑ **SOH CAH TOA** is an acronym that represents the right triangle relationships for sine, cosine, and tangent.

SOH: **S**in $\theta = \dfrac{\text{length of } \mathbf{O}\text{pposite side}}{\text{length of } \mathbf{H}\text{ypotenuse}}$

CAH: **C**os $\theta = \dfrac{\text{length of } \mathbf{A}\text{djacent side}}{\text{length of } \mathbf{H}\text{ypotenuse}}$

TOA: **T**an $\theta = \dfrac{\text{length of } \mathbf{O}\text{pposite side}}{\text{length of } \mathbf{A}\text{djacent side}}$

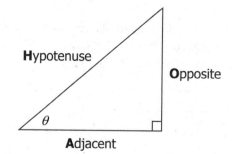

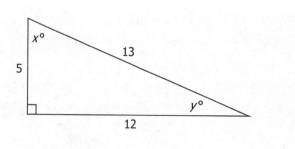

sin x = _____   cos y = _____   tan y = _____

❑ **Trig Identities** – Trig identities show the relationship between various trig functions. Know the following identities.

$\tan \theta = \dfrac{\sin \theta}{\cos \theta}$ $\sin^2 \theta + \cos^2 \theta = 1$

Complementary angle identities: $\cos A = \sin(90 - A)$ $\sin A = \cos(90 - A)$

Can you see how complementary angle identities are true by using SOHCAHTOA?

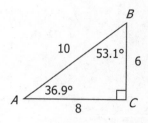

❑ **Degrees and Radians** – Angles can be measured in both degrees and radians. 180 degrees is equal to π radians.

To convert from radians to degrees, multiply by $\dfrac{180}{\pi}$.

To convert from degrees to radians multiply by $\dfrac{\pi}{180}$.

What is the value of 240° in radians? _____

What is the value of $\dfrac{\pi}{2}$ radians in degrees? _____

When using your calculator, make sure it is in the right mode: degrees or radians. If you are working on a trigonometry question and your calculator shows an answer that doesn't seem to make sense, check whether you are in the right mode.

❑ **The Unit Circle** – You won't have to fully understand the unit circle, but you should know how to use the unit circle to find the sine and cosine of common angles. Pay particular attention to the sign of cosine and sine in each of the quadrants.

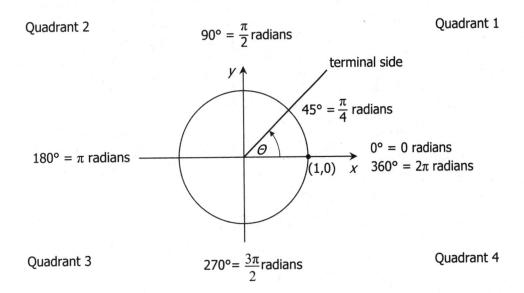

Quadrant 2

$90° = \dfrac{\pi}{2}$ radians

Quadrant 1

terminal side

$45° = \dfrac{\pi}{4}$ radians

$180° = \pi$ radians

θ

$0° = 0$ radians

$(1,0)$ x $360° = 2\pi$ radians

Quadrant 3

$270° = \dfrac{3\pi}{2}$ radians

Quadrant 4

❑ The value of the *x* and *y* coordinates where the **terminal** side of the angle intersects the unit circle equals the cosine and sine of the angle, respectively. Use SOH CAH TOA to see this concept.

The signs of the cosine functions in each quadrant mirror the signs of the *x* coordinates. Similarly, the signs of the sine functions mirror the signs of the *y* coordinates.

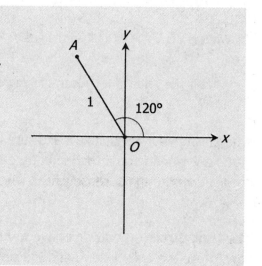

Terminal side $\overline{OA}$ has length of 1 unit.

Draw a right triangle with $\overline{OA}$ as the hypotenuse.

Using right triangle rules, find the other side lengths of the right triangle.

What are the coordinates of point *A*? _____

Find the sine and cosine of 120°.

cos 120° = _____

sin 120° = _____

❑ Know the following 1ˢᵗ and 2ⁿᵈ quadrant common sine and cosine values.

Angle Measure	Sine	Cosine
0° = 0 radians	0	1
$30° = \dfrac{\pi}{6}$ radians	$\dfrac{1}{2}$	$\dfrac{\sqrt{3}}{2}$
$45° = \dfrac{\pi}{4}$ radians	$\dfrac{\sqrt{2}}{2}$	$\dfrac{\sqrt{2}}{2}$
$60° = \dfrac{\pi}{3}$ radians	$\dfrac{\sqrt{3}}{2}$	$\dfrac{1}{2}$
$90° = \dfrac{\pi}{2}$ radians	1	0
$120° = \dfrac{2\pi}{3}$ radians	$\dfrac{\sqrt{3}}{2}$	$-\dfrac{1}{2}$
$135° = \dfrac{3\pi}{4}$ radians	$\dfrac{\sqrt{2}}{2}$	$-\dfrac{\sqrt{2}}{2}$
$150° = \dfrac{5\pi}{6}$ radians	$\dfrac{1}{2}$	$-\dfrac{\sqrt{3}}{2}$
180° = π radians	0	−1

PUT IT TOGETHER

1

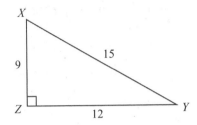

Given the triangle above, which of the following is equal to $\frac{3}{4}$?

A) $\sin X$

B) $\cos X$

C) $\cos Y$

D) $\tan Y$

2

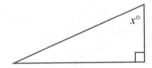

Note: Figure not drawn to scale.

In the triangle above, the cosine of $x°$ is $\frac{3}{7}$. What is the sine of $(90° - x°)$?

A) $\frac{3}{7}$

B) $\frac{4}{7}$

C) $\frac{2\sqrt{10}}{7}$

D) $2\sqrt{10}$

Complex Numbers

Occasionally, an SAT question will test your understanding of and ability to perform basic operations on complex numbers.

❑ The square root of a negative number is called an **imaginary number**. Imaginary numbers are expressed using i, which is defined to be $\sqrt{-1}$. So, $i = \sqrt{-1}$.

> Express the following in terms of i:
>
> $i^2 =$ $2i \times 5i =$

❑ The powers of i repeat in a cyclical pattern: $i, -1, -i, 1, i, -1, -i, 1,...$

Use this pattern to calculate higher powers of i.

$$i = \sqrt{-1} \qquad\qquad\qquad i^2 = -1$$

$$i^3 = \left(i^2 \cdot i\right) = (-1 \cdot i) = -i \qquad\qquad i^4 = \left(i^2 \cdot i^2\right) = (-1 \cdot -1) = 1$$

> $i^{14} =$ $i^{37} =$

❑ Simplify roots of negative numbers by using i.

> $\sqrt{-16} =$ $\sqrt{-50} =$

❑ A **complex number** is any number that can be expressed in the form of $a + bi$, where a and b are real numbers. All real numbers and all imaginary numbers can be expressed as complex numbers.

❑ **Add or subtract complex numbers** just as you would any two binomials – by combining like terms. To add or subtract complex numbers, simply add or subtract the real parts and add or subtract the imaginary parts.

$$6i + 5 - 2i + 3i =$$

❑ **Multiply complex numbers** just as you would any two binomials – either by distributing or by foiling. Remember that, when you multiply, you want to end up with a complex number in the form of $a + bi$.

$$3i - i(2i - 5) =$$ $$i(3 + i)(3 - i) =$$

❑ **Divide complex numbers** by multiplying the numerator and the denominator by the **complex conjugate** of the denominator. For example, if the denominator is $1 + 4i$, multiply the top and bottom of the fraction by $1 - 4i$. Remember when you divide complex numbers you want to end up with a complex number in the form of $a + bi$.

$$\frac{4 + i}{i}$$

Multiply top and bottom by $-i$:

$$\frac{1 - i}{2 + i}$$

Multiply top and bottom by $2 - i$:

Simplify:

PUT IT TOGETHER

1

Which of the following is equal to $2(2+i)-(6-7i)$?

(Note: $i=\sqrt{-1}$)

A) $10+9i$

B) $10-5i$

C) $-2+9i$

D) $-2-5i$

2

$$\frac{1+2i}{2-i}$$

Which of the following complex numbers is equivalent to the expression above when written in the form $a+bi$, where a and b are real numbers? (Note: $i=\sqrt{-1}$)

A) i

B) $\dfrac{2}{5}+i$

C) $\dfrac{4}{5}+i$

D) $\dfrac{4}{5}+\dfrac{3i}{5}$

> Solve this both with and without your calculator.
>
> When allowed, your calculator can help you solve complex number problems. Make sure your calculator is in "*a + bi*" mode and use parentheses to follow order of operations.

Additional Topics in Math Summary

- ❑ **Reference Information** – Do your best to memorize the formulas and rules given at the beginning of every SAT Math section.

- ❑ **Right angle** = 90°

- ❑ **Straight line angle** = 180°

- ❑ **Sum of interior angles of triangle** = 180°

- ❑ **Parallel Lines** – When a line crosses through parallel lines, it creates several sets of equal angles and supplementary angles.

- ❑ In an **isosceles** triangle, two sides are equal, and the two angles opposite those sides are equal.

- ❑ **Pythagorean Theorem**: $a^2 + b^2 = c^2$

- ❑ **Similar triangles** have corresponding angles that are equal and corresponding sides that are proportional. Similar triangles have the same shape but not necessarily the same size. Solve similar triangle questions by setting up a proportion of side lengths.

- ❑ **Area of Sector** = $\dfrac{x}{360}\left(\pi r^2\right)$

- ❑ **Length of Arc** = $\dfrac{x}{360}\left(2\pi r\right)$

- ❑ **Center-Radius Equation of a Circle:** $(x - h)^2 + (y - k)^2 = r^2$

  In this form, (h, k) is the center and r is the radius.

- ❑ **Completing the Square** – Not all circle equations are given in "center-radius" form. In those cases, you'll have to "Complete the Square" to get the equation into "center-radius" form.

❑ **SOH CAH TOA** is an acronym that represents the right triangle relationships for sine, cosine, and tangent.

SOH: $\mathbf{Sin}\,\theta = \dfrac{\text{length of \textbf{O}pposite side}}{\text{length of \textbf{H}ypotenuse}}$

CAH: $\mathbf{Cos}\,\theta = \dfrac{\text{length of \textbf{A}djacent side}}{\text{length of \textbf{H}ypotenuse}}$

TOA: $\mathbf{Tan}\,\theta = \dfrac{\text{length of \textbf{O}pposite side}}{\text{length of \textbf{A}djacent side}}$

❑ $\tan\theta = \dfrac{\sin\theta}{\cos\theta}$

❑ $\sin^2\theta + \cos^2\theta = 1$

❑ **Complementary angle identities:** $\cos A = \sin(90 - A)$ $\qquad\qquad$ $\sin A = \cos(90 - A)$

❑ **Degrees and Radians** – Angles can be measured in both degrees and radians. 180 degrees is equal to π radians.

To convert from radians to degrees, multiply by $\dfrac{180}{\pi}$.

To convert from degrees to radians multiply by $\dfrac{\pi}{180}$.

❑ When using your calculator, make sure it is in the right mode: degrees or radians. If you are working on a trigonometry question and your calculator shows an answer that doesn't seem to make sense, check whether you are in the right mode.

❑ **The Unit Circle** – You won't have to fully understand the unit circle, but you should know how to use the unit circle to find the sine and cosine of common angles.

❑ The square root of a negative number is called an **imaginary number**. Imaginary numbers are expressed using i, which is defined to be $\sqrt{-1}$. So, $i = \sqrt{-1}$.

❑ A **complex number** is any number that can be expressed in the form of $a + bi$, where a and b are real numbers. All real numbers and all imaginary numbers can be expressed as complex numbers.

Additional Topics in Math Practice

Angles

Questions 1-2: E
Question 3: M

1

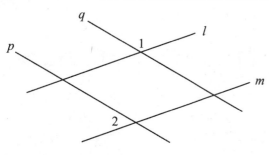

In the above figure, lines *l* and *m* are parallel and lines *p* and *q* are parallel. If the measure of ∠2 is 48°, what is the measure of ∠1?

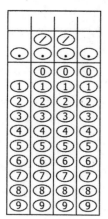

2

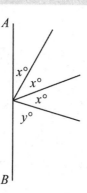

In the figure above, *AB* is a line segment, and $y = 2x$. What is the value of *y*?

A) 45
B) 68
C) 72
D) 84

3

The total number of degrees in a regular polygon can be determined using the formula Total Degrees = $(180)(n - 2)$, where *n* represents the number of sides of the polygon. What is the degree measure of each interior angle in a stop sign? (Note: a traditional stop sign has 8 sides of equal length).

A) 60
B) 90
C) 135
D) 175

Triangles

Questions 4-6: M

4

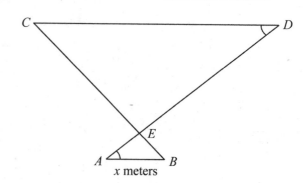

In the figure above, *AED* and *BEC* are straight lines and the measure of angle *EAB* is equal to the measure of angle *EDC*. If the lengths of segments *AE*, *BE*, *CE*, and *CD* are equal to 500 meters, 400 meters, 1200 meters and 2100 meters respectively, what is the value of *x*?

5

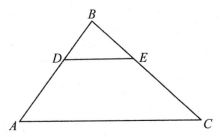

Note: Figure not drawn to scale.

In the figure above, if $\overline{DE} \parallel \overline{AC}$, which of the following proportions must be true?

A) $\dfrac{DA}{DE} = \dfrac{EC}{DE}$

B) $\dfrac{AC}{DE} = \dfrac{EC}{BE}$

C) $\dfrac{BE}{DE} = \dfrac{EC}{AC}$

D) $\dfrac{BE}{BC} = \dfrac{DE}{AC}$

6

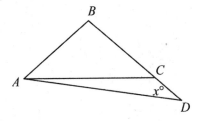

Note: Figure not drawn to scale

In the figure above, BCD is a line segment, $AB = 2$, $BC = 2$, and $AC = 2\sqrt{2}$. Which of the following could be a value of x?

A) 40
B) 45
C) 50
D) 65

Circles

Question 7:   E
Question 8:   M
Question 9:   H

7

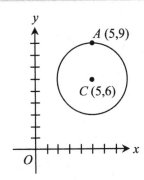

In the figure above, if A is a point on the circle with center C, what is the area of the circle?

A) 2π
B) 4π
C) 6π
D) 9π

8

A circle in the xy-plane is centered at $(-2, 0)$ and the endpoint of a radius passes through the point $\left(-1, \dfrac{12}{5}\right)$. What is an equation of the circle?

A) $(x+2)^2 + y^2 = \dfrac{169}{25}$

B) $(x-2)^2 + y^2 = \dfrac{169}{25}$

C) $(x+2)^2 + y^2 = \dfrac{13}{5}$

D) $(x-2)^2 + y^2 = \dfrac{13}{5}$

9

$$x^2 + y^2 + 6x - 12y = 11$$

The equation above defines a circle in the xy-plane. What are the coordinates of the center of the circle?

A) $(3,-6)$
B) $(-3,6)$
C) $(6,-3)$
D) $(-6,3)$

Volume

Question 10:   M

10

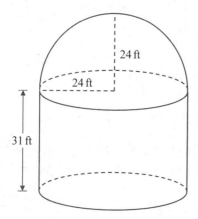

A water tower storage tank is made of a right circular cylinder and a hemisphere, with measures as shown above. Which of the following is closest to the volume, in cubic feet, of the storage tank?

A) $61,211 \text{ ft}^3$

B) $85,049 \text{ ft}^3$

C) $93,484 \text{ ft}^3$

D) $114,002 \text{ ft}^3$

Trigonometry

Questions 11-12:   E
Question 13:   M

11

In a right triangle, one angle measures $x°$, where $\cos x° = \dfrac{3}{5}$. What is $\sin(90° - x°)$?

A) $-\dfrac{4}{5}$

B) $-\dfrac{3}{5}$

C) $\dfrac{3}{5}$

D) $\dfrac{4}{5}$

12

If $\theta = \dfrac{19\pi}{12}$ radians, what is the value of θ in degrees?

A) 285
B) 300
C) 465
D) 570

13

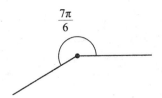

$$\frac{7\pi}{6}$$

Which of the following is the cosine of the angle shown above?

A) $\dfrac{\sqrt{3}}{2}$

B) $-\dfrac{\sqrt{3}}{2}$

C) $-\dfrac{\sqrt{2}}{2}$

D) $-\dfrac{1}{2}$

Complex Numbers

Question 14:   M
Question 15:   H

 14

For the imaginary number i such that $i = \sqrt{-1}$, which of the following is equal to
$i(3-4i) - 2i(1+2i)$?

A) $8 + 5i$
B) $8 + i$
C) $5i$
D) i

15

$$\frac{4+i}{3+i^2} \div \frac{4-i}{3-i^2}$$

Which of the following complex numbers is equivalent to the expression above?

(Note: $i = \sqrt{-1}$)

A) $\dfrac{32}{15} + \dfrac{16i}{15}$

B) $\dfrac{30}{17} + \dfrac{16i}{17}$

C) $2 + \dfrac{16i}{15}$

D) $2 + \dfrac{16i}{17}$

Miscellaneous

Questions 16-17: E
Questions 18-20: M
Questions 21-22: H

 16

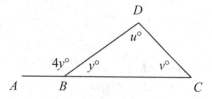

In the figure above, B lies on $\overline{AC}$. What is the value of $u + v$?

A) 90
B) 100
C) 132
D) 144

Category: _____

 17

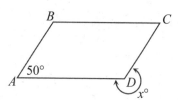

In the figure above, if $ABCD$ is a parallelogram, what is the value of x?

A) 130
B) 200
C) 230
D) 250

Category: _____

 18

In the figure above, two right triangles share a common side. If $AB = 5$, $BD = 12$, and $CD = 3\sqrt{3}$, what is the length of $\overline{AC}$?

A) 14
B) $8\sqrt{3}$
C) 13
D) $3\sqrt{10}$

Category: _____

19

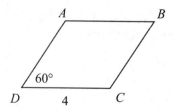

$ABCD$ is a parallelogram. If $\overline{AC}$ is drawn so that it bisects $\angle BAD$, what is the length of $\overline{AC}$?

A) $2\sqrt{3}$
B) 4
C) $4\sqrt{2}$
D) $4\sqrt{3}$

Category: _____

SUMMIT
EDUCATIONAL
GROUP

20

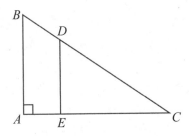

In the figure above $\overline{AB} \parallel \overline{DE}$. If $AB = 8$, $AE = 3$, and $EC = 9$, what is the length of $\overline{DE}$?

A) $4\dfrac{1}{2}$

B) 6

C) $6\dfrac{1}{4}$

D) 8

Category: _____

21

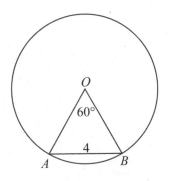

In the figure above, O is the center of the circle. What is the area of $\triangle AOB$?

A) $2\sqrt{3}$

B) $3\sqrt{3}$

C) $4\sqrt{3}$

D) $8\sqrt{2}$

Category: _____

22

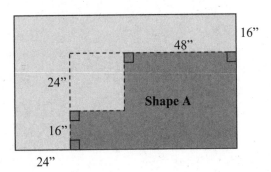

The diagram above shows the pattern for cutting Shape A from a rectangular 56"×96" plywood board. What is the area, in square inches, of the amount of the plywood board that is NOT used in Shape A?

A) 2,304 square inches
B) 2,688 square inches
C) 2,880 square inches
D) 3,072 square inches

Category: _____

SUMMIT
EDUCATIONAL
GROUP

Answer Key

MATH OVERVIEW

Problem-Solving Tools

p. 17

  C

  Check your answer by plugging values for x and y back into the equations.

  x is equal to 4, and y is equal to 1

  $y - x$ is equal to -3

Plugging In

p. 18

  C

  C

Choosing Numbers

p. 19

  Try 100

  16 days, decays by 50% twice, 125 g remaining

  D

  A

Using Your Calculator

p. 21

  $-5^2 = -25$

  $(-5)^2 = 25$

  $\dfrac{-6 \times 20}{4 \times 5} = -6$

  $\dfrac{2}{3} - \dfrac{1}{5} = 7/15$

  $\dfrac{52}{455} = 4/35$

  When $x = 1.5$, $y = -1.75$

  x-interepts = 2, -2

  $f(x)$ and $g(x)$ intersect twice

  Intersections: (-1,-3) (2,0)

PROBLEM SOLVING AND DATA ANALYSIS

Percents – Part 1

p. 28

  22% of 110 = 24.2

  12 is what percent of 15? 80%

  Value for sodium: 100

  Sodium content of "Reduced Sodium": 80

  Sodium content of "Salt & Vinegar": 120

  Compare values: 150%

p. 29 Put It together

  1. A

  2. C

  3. C

Percents – Part 2

p. 30

  Percent markdown: 25%

  Population: 13949

  Bill: B

  Tip: 0.18B

  Total Bill: 1.18B

  Cost of parts: $617.75

  Counteroffer: 88%

p. 31 Put It Together

  1. C

  2. D

  3. B

Ratios
p. 32

Apples to oranges: 2 to 3

Apples: 3/5

Number of apples: 18

5 picked: 3 apples, 2 oranges

Faster car: 120 miles in 3 hours

Jar with largest ratio: Sharon's

p. 33 Put It Together
1. D
2. B
3. A

Proportions
p. 34

$n = 2$

$n = 9.3$

$n = 4$

$x = 56.32$

Continent to move 1000 feet: 15,385 years

p. 35 Put It Together
1. C
2. C
3. B

Units and Conversion
p. 36

Ounces in 2 gallons: 256

Square centimeters: 7600

p. 37 Put It Together
1. D
2. D
3. B

Checkpoint Review – p. 38
1. C
2. B
3. B
4. C
5. B
6. D

Statistics – Average (Mean)
p. 40

Average temperature: 63°

Sum: 72

Gala apples: $3 \times 16 = 48$

Honeycrisp apples: $4 \times 23 = 92$

Total: 140

Average: 20

p. 41 Put It Together
1. B
2. D
3. C

Statistics – Median, Mode, and Range
p. 42

Median of List A: 17

Median of List B: 19.5

Mode: 37, 38

Range: 59

Standard Deviation of {89, 90, 92} is less than that of {80, 90, 100}

p. 43 Put It Together
1. A
2. A
3. C

Data Relationships
p. 44

Data correlation: strong

Data correlation: negative

Distance: 2 km

Largest increase: 2008

General trend: increasing

p. 46 Put It Together
1. C
2. B
3. D
4. B
5. B

Data Collection and Conclusions
p. 49 Put It Together
1. B
2. C
3. B

Problem Solving and Data Analysis Practice
p. 54
1. D
2. A
3. B
4. C
5. B
6. D
7. 36
8. C
9. D
10. D
11. D
12. C
13. B
14. D
15. 0
16. D
17. D
18. D
19. D
20. C
21. B
22. 4/7
23. D
24. C
25. D
26. B
27. B
28. C
29. B
30. B

HEART OF ALGEBRA

Algebraic Expressions
p. 64
$k^2 - 3k + 5$
$-6x^2 - 3x + 9$
$x^2 + 4x - 5$
$3x^2(x - 2)^2$

p. 65 Put It Together
1. A
2. A
3. C

Algebraic Equations & Inequalities
p. 66
$x = 2$
$x = 6$

$15 - a = 10$
$x > -4$
$x = 4$: NO
$x = -2$: NO
$x = -4$: YES
A

p. 68 Put It Together
1. D
2. A
3. B
4. D
5. D

Absolute Value
p. 70
2
2
x
$-x$
9
5
$5 < x < 9$
$x < 5$ or $x > 9$

p. 71 Put It Together
1. D
2. C

Systems of Linear Equations
p. 72
infinite solutions
when simplified, they are the same equation
multiply by 2
$y = -3$
$y = -2x + 3$
$x = 3$
S = number of sweaters sold
$12T + 25S = 309$
$T = 7$

p. 74 Put It Together
1. B
2. B
3. 32
4. B

Checkpoint Review – p. 76
1. C
2. D
3. D
4. ½
5. D

Slope
p. 78
  −2/3
  Undefined
  −2/3
  3/2
  0

p. 79 Put It Together
1. A
2. D
3. C

Graphs of Linear Equations
p. 80
  Standard Form
  $y = 3x − 7/2$
  slope = 3
  y-intercept = −7/2
  x-intercept = 7/6
  $y = 3x$
  $y = −x/3$
  slope = −1/2
  $y = − (1/2)x + b$
  $b = 1/2$

p. 81 Put It Together
1. C
2. D
3. C
4. C
5. A

Graphs of Linear Inequalities
p. 85 Put It Together
1. B

Creating Linear Models
p. 86
  $70
  c
  $0.22c + 70$
  $E = 0.22c + 10h$
  3000 ft
  1400 ft
  D

p. 87 Put It Together
1. B
2. C
3. A

Interpreting Linear Models
p. 88
  h = hours after passing rail switch
  d increases by 60
  d = distance from station
  3
  3 = distance from station to switch
  $d = 2t + 8$
  d = total depth of snow
  t = number of hours snow has fallen since 1am
  slope = 2
  2 = additional inches of snow each hour
  d-intercept = 8
  8 = inches of snow at 1am

p. 90 Put It Together
1. B
2. A
3. D
4. D

Heart of Algebra Practice – p. 96
1. C
2. B
3. A
4. D
5. 6
6. D
7. D
8. B
9. A
10. D
11. A
12. D
13. C
14. 7/11
15. C

16. A
17. D
18. C
19. A
20. A
21. A
22. 16
23. A
24. C
25. 76
26. B
27. A
28. D
29. D
30. C
31. B
32. D
33. A
34. 6
35. C

PASSPORT TO ADVANCED MATH

Equations with Fractions

p. 106

$x = 3/2$

$x = 4$

$x = 2$

p. 107 Put It Together

1. D
2. D
3. D

Equations with Exponents

p. 108

2^7

x^3

x^6

$1/27$

$1/9$

$125x^6y^3$

1

99

$a = 1$

p. 109 Put It Together

1. C
2. B
3. C

Equations with Radicals

p. 110

2

3

6

9/5

1/8

$\sqrt[3]{x} = 2/4$

$x = 1/8$

p. 111 Put It Together

1. C
2. D
3. C

Checkpoint Review – p. 112

1. D
2. B
3. D
4. B

Functions

p. 114

$f(3) = 4$

$f(a) = a^2 - 5$

$x^2 - 2x - 4$

5 and −5

$f(g(3)) = 29$

$g(f(3)) = 167$

$g(f(x + 1)) = 16x^2 + 40x + 23$

p. 115 Put It Together

1. B
2. C
3. D

Graphs of Functions

p. 116

$f(0) = 3$

$f(-2) = 2$

$f(x) = 2.5$ twice

p. 117 Put It Together

1. B
2. C
3. C
4. A

Quadratic Equations

p. 120

$$x^2 - 5x + 6 = 0$$
$$(x - 3)(x - 2) = 0$$
$$x - 3 = 0 \quad x - 2 = 0$$
$$x = 3 \quad x = 2$$
$$x = \frac{-5 \pm \sqrt{17}}{4}$$

Because you take the square root of the discriminant, you can use root rules to determine the types of solutions for a quadratic.

p. 122 Put It Together
1. D
2. A
3. C
4. A
5. A

Graphs of Quadratics

p. 125

$$y + 8 = 2x^2 + 12x$$
$$y + 8 = 2(x^2 + 6x)$$
$$y + 8 + 18 = 2(x^2 + 3x + 9)$$
$$y = 2(x + 3)^2 - 26$$
vertex = (−3, −26)

p. 126 Put It Together
1. B
2. A
3. D

Polynomials

p. 128

x-intercept of $P(x) = (6,0)$
one factor is $(x - 6)$
zeros of $P(x) = 3, -1, 0$
x-intercepts of $P(x) = (3,0)\ (-1,0)\ (0,0)$
value of P when $x = -3$ is 0
$P(x) = x^3 - 3x^2 - x + 3$
$x = 0, -2, -3$
$x = -2$
factors = $(x - 2)\ (x^2 + 2x - 8)$
zeros = $x = 2, -4$

p. 130 Put It Together
1. A
2. C
3. A
4. D
5. B

Nonlinear Models

p. 132

10,000 represents the original population
1.3 represents the 30% weekly increase
week 4 population is 28,561
week 10 population is 137,858
4 represents the initial height
after 1.875 seconds
max height = 18.0625 feet

p. 134 Put It Together
1. D
2. C
3. C

Passport to Advanced Math Practice – p. 140
1. C
2. 1
3. A
4. B
5. C
6. 1
7. B
8. 3
9. B
10. B
11. B
12. D
13. A
14. C
15. A
16. B
17. D
18. A
19. A
20. D
21. B
22. B
23. A
24. C
25. A
26. B
27. A
28. D
29. C
30. A
31. 2/3
32. C

ADDITIONAL TOPICS IN MATH

Angles

p. 151

$x = 90$

$a + b + c + d = 360$

$a = c, b = d$

$x + y + z = 180$

$a + b + c + d = 360$

$a + b + c + d + e = 540$

$a = 108$

p. 153 Put It Together

1. A
2. D
3. A

Triangles

p. 154

area = $bh/2$

perimeter = $b + c + d$

missing legs: $\sqrt{73}$, 3

proportion = $6/9 = 10/s$

$s = 15$

angles are equal

twice the length ($2x$)

yes, they are similar, because they have equal angles created by parallel lines and intersecting lines

p. 156 Put It Together

1. 24
2. D

Circles

p. 158

area = πr^2

circumference = $2\pi r$

diameter = $2r$

$\pi \approx 3.14...$

arc AB: 4π

sector AOB: 12π

$x^2 + (y - 3)^2 = 16$

center = $(1, -3)$

radius = 6

p. 160 Put It Together

1. A
2. B
3. D

Volume

p. 162

72.257 cubic meters

p. 163 Put It Together

1. 54
2. C

Trigonometry

p. 164

$\sin x = 12/13$

$\cos y = 12/13$

$\tan y = 5/12$

$240° = 4\pi/3$ radians

$\pi/2$ radians $= 90°$

A coordinates are $\left(-\dfrac{1}{2}, \dfrac{\sqrt{3}}{2} \right)$

$\cos 120° = \left(-\dfrac{1}{2} \right)$

$\sin 120° = \left(\dfrac{\sqrt{3}}{2} \right)$

p. 167 Put It Together

1. D
2. A

Complex Numbers

p. 168

-1

-10

-1

i

$4i$

$5i\sqrt{2}$

$7i + 5$

$2 + 8i$

$10i$

$1 - 4i$

$\dfrac{1 - 3i}{5}$

p. 170 Put It Together

1. C
2. A

Additional Topics in Math Practice – p. 176

1. 132
2. C
3. C
4. 700
5. D
6. A
7. D
8. A
9. B
10. B
11. C
12. A
13. B
14. B
15. B
16. D
17. C
18. A
19. B
20. B
21. C
22. D

Test Week Checklist

Week of the Test

❏ You worked hard. Feel confident that you are prepared for the test. If you want to study more, review the Chapter Summaries, but do not try to cram at the last minute. By now, you know what you know.

❏ Take it easy, and get good sleep throughout the week. You want to be well rested for test day.

❏ If you are not testing at your own school, make sure you know where you're going. Don't rely on an online mapping program the morning of the test. If you need to, take a test run the weekend before.

Friday night

❏ Again, you know what you know. Do something relaxing and fun.

❏ Lay out everything you need to bring with you:

- Your admission ticket

- Official photo ID

- 3 or 4 sharpened No. 2 pencils with erasers

- Approved calculator with new batteries (check the College Board website for a list of approved calculator models)

- Watch

- Water (the College Board allows you to bring a clear bottle with the label removed)

- A small snack that won't get your hands sticky

❏ Visualize success. See yourself solving question after question. Envision completing the last question, putting your pencil down, and closing the test booklet. Let yourself feel the good feeling of a job well done.

❏ Go to sleep at the same time you've been going to sleep all week. Otherwise, you'll just toss and turn. Don't worry if you have trouble sleeping. You'll have plenty of adrenaline to keep your brain going during the test.

Test Week Checklist

Morning of the Test

❑ Have a backup alarm – either another clock or a parent.

❑ Eat a good breakfast. Make sure to avoid heavy, fatty foods.

❑ Do something easy that you enjoy (take a walk or listen to music). You want to go into the test awake and upbeat.

At the Test

❑ Arrive early to the test center to find your room and settle in.

❑ Make sure to use the bathroom before you start the test. You only have a few short breaks during the test; you don't want to have to worry about a line at the restroom.

❑ Find your seat and sit for a minute. Continue to visualize yourself working successfully through the test, using all of the skills and strategies you've learned. You're ready!

❑ During breaks, stand up and walk around. It helps you to stay focused.

❑ Pace yourself and keep your eye on the clock.

❑ If you start losing focus, try this concentration exercise: Every five questions, put down your pencil, stare at the ceiling, blink a few times, take several deep, slow breaths and then continue with the next five questions.

After the Test

❑ Plan to do something positive and fun. You deserve it!